37

The Year I Stopped Making Excuses,

embraced my power

& Launched My Million-Dollar Business

Aly Sterling

37: THE YEAR I STOPPED MAKING EXCUSES, EMBRACED MY POWER AND LAUNCHED MY MILLION-DOLLAR BUSINESS

ISBN-13: 978-0-578-66432-3

Printed in the United States of America

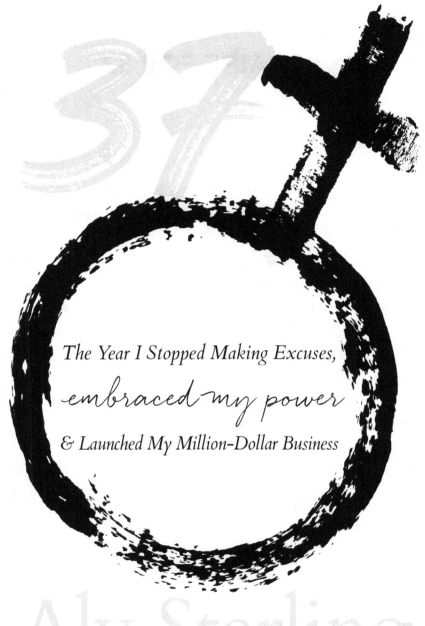

37

The Year I Stopped Making Excuses,

embraced my power

& Launched My Million-Dollar Business

Aly Sterling

*"I learned from Aly that efficiency is a must, how to stop apologizing - like most women do -
and position ourselves as the experts we are, and to think big; if it doesn't exist, create it."*
-Jenny Goldberg Perin

PRAISE FOR 37 ☿

"Empowered women not only uplift communities, they inspire other women to do the same.

As a friend, mentor, and confidant, Aly has been a source of wisdom and guidance that has allowed me to push past self-adopted limitations and propel both my personal and professional life to new levels. I am guilty of getting caught up in the perpetual cycle of 'getting ready to get ready,' whether it's launching new ideas or dealing with situations and circumstances in running a small business. Aly's gift of tuning into 'what is not being said' and asking thought-provoking questions has created momentum in my life in a way that have given me growth and new potential. Thank you, Aly, for empowering me!"

-Leslie Chapman, owner Toledo Yoga

PRAISE FOR 37

"I have seen Aly build her business from a handful of local clients to a nationwide presence. As her mentee since 2007, I have learned that efficiency is a must, how to stop apologizing - like most women do - and position ourselves as the experts we are, and to think big; if it doesn't exist, create it. It is Aly's influence that got me over my closet-full of excuses to start my own business."

–Jenny Goldberg Perin, Aly Sterling Philanthropy Senior Advisor and Integrative Nutrition Health Coach and Founder, Shift Life Health Coaching

"Aly Sterling shares the beautiful elements of a successful company, accolades earned, and honors bestowed from professional colleagues. However, the guts of 37, and what Aly wants the reader to leave with, is the complex, messy, and hidden surprises - more like WTF moments - faced when launching a business. 37 walks readers through the weeds of the unknown with humor, honesty, and humility. As a woman and entrepreneur, 37 is a guide to share with the tribe, re-read when frustrated and defeated, and use to celebrate our inner Aly when we nail it."

–Jen Skeldon, President, J.Skeldon Consulting Partners

"In true Aly fashion, she has given a gift to us by writing a book that is thoughtful, useful, easy to read, and has the perfect balance of encouragement and humility. 37 is relatable, action-oriented, and, most importantly, provides the reader with the confidence we've all been looking for. Her dedication to her business, this book, and empowering women is inspiring to all. Her strong work ethic, thoughtful and realistic approach are the foundation for all she has accomplished."

–Liz Vetter, President & Founder, Vibe Inc.

To my three brilliant girls, Madeline, Amelia and Gabrielle,
everything, always and forever, is for you.

To my mother and father,
both of whom did not let their pasts define them.

To Jonathan,
I always knew you were real.

Contents

introduction

At age forty-six, I won a regional Entrepreneur of the Year award, and as I stood in front of a crowd of five-hundred people, getting ready to accept my award and give a quick speech, I quietly began to laugh - at myself. You know, that nervous laugh; the one you hope like hell no one notices; the kind that awkwardly comes out when you learn of the death of someone. It's not that you find death funny, but, for some reason, when faced with something really uncomfortable and surprising, your limbic brain takes over and manifests in a big smile. In this situation, it was more of a *I-think-they-have-this-wrong* laugh. Boy, had I fooled those judges.

When I was drafting my speech, I reflected on what it was like to struggle as a "Jill of all trades" growing up—never excelling in any one thing and being insanely jealous of those who did. What I didn't realize is that grey space is fertile ground for a budding entrepreneur. Life becomes one big petri dish with a mind-numbing amount of (healthy and dangerous) combinations to play around with. Fortunately, as I sifted my way through countless crazy ideas (tween nail salon, anyone?) and many back-of-the-cocktail-napkin ill-fated business plans, finally - *finally!* - at the age of thirty-seven, I became a real, live adult and settled on just one of them. And my business was born.

But what a messy, dirty, and unscripted thirty-six years it had been getting there. What I didn't expect was that the even harder part was the next ten years of raising this baby (and in this situation, you can call the baby ugly - it was at first).

I drafted the end of my speech and reflected that there's no online business plan tutorial or MBA that will truly equip us, especially those of us who are women, to be prepared for the emotional rollercoaster ride you just strapped yourself into when launching a business. From the

> **There's no online business plan tutorial or MBA that will truly equip us, especially those of us who are women, to be prepared for the emotional rollercoaster ride you just strapped yourself into when launching a business.**

fear of leaving a stable job for the great financial unknown, to having to over-justify your business idea in a way men don't have to, to the constant guilt associated with leaving your kids at the sitter longer than the other moms, to realizing you have to walk away from people in your life who are just. plain. toxic., including your best friends and possibly your husband or wife. I wish these emotional truths weren't real, but they are, and every bit as sidelining as not having a marketing plan or line of credit or good website. You can have all of those things, but if you don't have a strong sense of self and thick skin, there's no amount EBITA (Earnings Before Interest, Taxes, and Amortization) that will save you.

Look forward to the day when the thrill of saying *yes* will outweigh the fear of saying *no*. You'll know when you have arrived, and there will be no looking back. All the crazy ideas you've had will simmer down to one. And you'll grow three inches taller in one day - ready and able to hang that shingle.

But before you reach that quickly approaching day, be sure to put your own air mask on first because you are going to need the extra oxygen to make it through to standing up on that podium and winning your own award someday. Everyone will encounter their own unique version of my orange barrels—trust me, they'll show up someday and create quite an emotional traffic jam. **So, my hope is that by sharing my personal experiences, my messy and dirty orange barrels, you won't be blindsided by the ones that surface for you. Instead, you'll see those barrels before they get close enough to slow you down, or you'll see them and drive right through them (rockstar!), or, if you're like most of us, you'll find a different route to success to take, possibly avoiding them altogether. It's the missing chapter in most MBA required reading books: the unique experience of the female entrepreneur.**

Ten years later, within the blink of an eye, your business baby grows up, and so do you. While you both look a little less messy, and a little less dirty, life is still radically unscripted. But unlike before, you have learned to thrive in the Land of Unscripted. It suits you quite well and has resulted in a business with amazing clients and employees and reputation. And you'll do what I did as I delivered my speech that day: You'll get over yourself and stop nervously laughing for a moment, you will graciously accept the recognition (that you absolutely know you deserve), you'll thank everyone from your second grade teacher to that dick who asked if your business was a hobby, and, within minutes, you'll begin thinking about the next crazy idea that has been simmering in your head. Only, this time, you won't doubt yourself as much and everyone will take you a bit more seriously, which should make you feel less restless, but like a shark who needs to constantly move, slowing down is not an option.

one

NEVER STOP MOVING

*"It's nice to be important,
but it is more important to be nice."
-John, retired art museum security guard
and early mentor of mine*

I'll start with the truth.
I had imaginary friends for way longer than you are supposed to.

We moved far too often – at least every two years when I was growing up. Just as I would get to know my neighbors and their kids, we would find a new, shinier house, pack up and move. We weren't moving to escape a debt collector or because either of my parents had committed some crime or transgression, but simply because my parents found a nicer home or subdivision. My dad was in the mortgage industry and knew how to time things. And my mom was all about new scenery and floorplans and, at that time (and maybe still today), that meant moving into a better neighborhood, even if it was in the same town and often only a few miles away. By my sister's count, we moved seventeen times before she graduated high school. Again, no, we were not evading the law.

We also had a new car every year or so. New homes, new cars. Essentially, my feet were never firmly planted. I could never feel settled or at ease for long. The scenery was always changing and shifting, and much like my spirit animal, the shark, I never stopped moving.

Left to my own devices, and learning quickly not to get too close to the neighbors, I imagined my friends. Mostly, I imagined Jonathan, my "husband."

I loved, loved, loved Jonathan. He went with me everywhere (of course he did – he was invisible). I actually made my family reserve a seat for him at the table for dinner, including Thanksgiving, and, oddly enough, they did. How generous was that? Jonathan and my friends hung out with me (my friends were never given names – not sure what that was all about) and kept me company from the time I was probably four or five until I was nine or ten. I can't be exactly sure, but I do know I was self-aware enough to know I was being ridiculous, like that kid who is still sucking their thumb in middle school.

When I'm asked what utility Jonathan held for me, I know it had everything to do with the fact I didn't have real friends around me. My sister was nearly five years younger than me (and I was completely disinterested in her), and in between hosting parties, my parents fought a lot. I'd find myself in my bedroom, in my own world, very often—but I liked it there. I knew my imaginary friends and husband wouldn't hurt me, and I wouldn't hurt them. They needed me as much as I needed them.

My active imagination didn't stop there. Inspired by books like

Manx Mouse and *The Lion, the Witch and the Wardrobe*, I created story after story about alternate universes that existed down the street from my grandparents' home along the river—elaborate picnics with sea creatures and damsels in distress. My mind never slowed down. But the problem was exactly that – I existed inside my head, and knew that was not a sustainable way to grow up.

I found solace in pretending, in the imaginary, in what was not available to me today, but what is possible tomorrow. And while growing up often felt lonely, it taught me invaluable lessons in self-reliance, creativity, and the art of making the best out of every situation. I was just as restless then as I am now, and though my imaginary friends have disappeared, I carry with me the things they taught me. I haven't stopped moving yet, always swimming towards the possibilities that tomorrow might bring.

Now, I get the most restless and can't sleep when things are good. Like, really good. Numbers are strong, the pipeline is healthy, turnover is low, and the team is productive and energetic. That's when I should be celebrating, but instead, I start to worry.

Sure, there's probably a proper diagnosis out there somewhere that can explain this glitch in me—maybe it's that I can't be happy (not a chance) or am paranoid (nope) or it could just be that I've read one too many case studies of the bad things that happen when leaders and creators step back too long to gloat. Bad things happen. Think Enron. Or the entire taxicab industry. In my little corner of the world, I've watched it play out – usually when someone builds too fast, or relies too heavily on a handful of big clients or treats their corporate account as their personal account. Any way you slice it, it happens a lot, and it often doesn't end well.

So, you'll never stop moving because you are in constant search mode for your next client and you can never assume a contract means anything (because, unfortunately, unless you want to incur an amount similar or more than the amount of the contract in legal fees, most likely, you will not enforce the terms). When you score a big win, celebrate and whoop and holler, but then ask your business manager (or yourself) to pretend as if only a portion of it exists. Don't staff up to it. Instead, bonus bigger at the end of the year and challenge your team to apply the 25% rule by letting go of what they don't need to be doing to free up more client time.

There's always more time to be created. My team has told me more than once that they don't have the time to take on one more client (and I, too, have felt this way). When I gently push back and ask to look under the hood, it's not difficult for me to find where they've normalized a slower pace when we weren't as busy, or added unnecessary adminis-trivia to their day, or, in my case, taken on extra pro bono tasks for a cause I love. Resetting all of those things will uncover the 25% needed to say yes to more paying work. And for at least most of us, we need to get paid.

It is a bitter pill to acknowledge that how you built your business a few years ago will not be how you grow or even maintain your business a few years from now. I wish I could tell you it would be, as we could put more on autopilot and go about realizing new dreams, but there is no autopilot for an organic, living, breathing ecosystem reliant on sustenance and constantly at risk. I think the same can be said for anything important in life. We shouldn't assume our personal relationships are in a "coast" mode either, should we? We have to constantly be working to make them better, to hedge the odds, to anticipate change and forecast growth. That's why we never stop moving.

> **Your industry will change.**
> **Your staff will change.**
> **You will change.**
> Let me explain more.

I don't need to say much about why your industry will change. It should be abundantly obvious that everything changes today, and quicker than ever before. If you aren't spending a lot of your time watching and researching the trends associated with your industry, what your competitors are doing, surveying your clients and past clients to learn about how their needs have changed, you need to do so. I think about this all. the. time.

How your staff may change is far more nuanced. In my experience, our firm's needs have outgrown some of my team's abilities. Many joined our firm at a point in time when both our needs were small, and their bandwidth and expertise were perfectly aligned. Take, for instance, my original marketing manager who was terrific at helping to proofread, create copy for collateral, and work with vendors to establish our first website, as well as produce direct mail materials. Fast forward a few years and we now have three offices and a national presence that requires a competitive social media strategy, investment in an SEO platform, and a public relations strategy to court media time. She did not possess those skills nor, frankly, was she interested in learning them. It takes a lot of intuition and a structured approach to mapping strategy and mission to your team members' current and desired skills - via constant performance evaluations and straightforward heart-to-hearts over a few glasses of wine - to know when things are not growing in the same direction.

And you. I was very surprised when the moment occurred that I knew I was no longer interested in playing the same role in the firm as the day I founded it. For some silly reason, I thought I would always be content doing about 30% leadership and business-building and 70% service delivery (by the way, even that ratio is untenable—the only reason it worked was because I was working eighty-hour weeks). I wanted to spend 70% of my time looking forward, leading, and motivating my team, but, somehow, I think that sounded like too much fun, so it didn't seem like work, per se—that killing myself doing both for the rest of my life was what everyone else did. And then I woke up, thought big, and built my way into where I am today, which is that 70/30 ratio, with a new division ready to launch and this book forthcoming. Remember, we are our own worst enemies, creating and buying into our limiting beliefs about what is possible.

Early success is a wonderful thing for those of us it happens to. It can catapult you forward and, done well, you can leverage it in many positive ways. It can also create a false or selective memory of how you got there and allow you to overlook the mistakes you surmounted as well as the people who helped along the way. And then you know what can happen… you are at risk of developing an unhealthy ego. A healthy ego is okay. It actually allows us to separate our interests from someone else's, which can be extremely advantageous in business, but an outsized ego can be a massive turn-off to your clients, prospective clients, and team.

I'm thankful that I'm really a shy introvert who manages to perform well when I need to. I've been able to crawl out of my skin and muster the nerve and the stamina to speak in front of crowds of twenty to seven hundred. Each time I do, no matter the crowd size (yet amplified when it is bigger), I get nervous and question my abilities, and then, afterwards, no matter the high-fives and glowing evals I receive, I doubt myself. I think that they were just being nice (or, conversely, that the other speakers were boring)—that somehow, I'm still not good enough. And while my close friends tell me I need to get over this because I am everything the reviews and comments point to, I don't want to get over this part of my flaws. I don't know how being completely confident would improve me or make me better. I am afraid I would lose this self-deprecating air I have about me (which is not an act, it is my natural default state) that seems to work just fine.

The quote I cited at the beginning of this chapter was from an elderly security guard who used to sit outside the museum gift shop I worked in when I was in high school. He would tell me about what he used to do for a living, about his deceased wife, about his children who lived far away in different states, but who made a point to call him weekly and visit as often as they could. John was a very happy and satisfied man who loved his part-time job protecting valuable art and having conversations with strangers.

John told me so many stories about his interactions with visitors: How he could tell a nice person from a not-so-nice person. How they spoke to him, how they spoke and interacted with anyone they were with, how our body language and how we hold ourselves (posture, gaze, arm positioning) can say a lot about our accomplishments and our fears.

It would be insincere for me to say I remember many of his stories. I don't. But I do remember the mood he created for me and the residual glow that has lasted many decades. The principle that he shared framed and guides who I was, am, and hopefully will continue to be: *it is nice to be important, but it is more important to be nice.* I wonder if John ever thought I'd keep that front and center in my life all of these years.

> **Keeping kindness in the forefront allows us to be present for the amazing and unplanned power of how all the little things we do add up in magical ways.**

It was John's sentiment that has encouraged me to remain open to learning opportunities of all kinds, and one of those opportunities came through a sweet soul named Ruby.

I'm a big fan of art—all kinds of art, including some of the best art that is created by people with developmental differences. One of my favorite studios is a local one that is affiliated with a longstanding non-profit that serves the needs of acute and independent developmentally different and autistic people. It is amazing, and I am constantly buying art for my home and office and as gifts for everyone. Each artist is a client of the nonprofit, and as part of their daily therapy, they create and, in turn, receive income from their sales. You cannot go in there without falling in love—with far more than the art.

I have three framed pieces of artwork in my office, one sculptural piece in our foyer, and an abstract wall-hanging in our staff lounge. Now, our office is not big - maybe 2,500 square feet - and in that space there are five pieces of artwork from this studio. It makes our space even more cheery and welcoming.

Our fabulous landlord has always had a strong social service connection - being a volunteer, serving on boards and as a philanthropic partner in the community. As part of that commitment, he switched cleaning companies to one that is operated by the same developmentally different nonprofit, which also has a workforce development arm, including commercial cleaning.

As part of this switch, our landlord informed us that we would have a new cleaning team, and that it might take them a little extra time to acclimate to the office and our particular needs. Also, that the crew might be a bit more bashful than others in the past because this team, with the exception of the team leader who would leave after dropping them off and giving them their coaching session, would be completely new to their role and responsibility. Plus, they might not be used to working after 5 p.m. and by themselves. So, essentially, cut them some slack.

One evening after 5 p.m., I was alone in the building and ran into our new cleaning team member outside in the main foyer, on my way to the restroom. As I passed by her and her cart full o' cleaning goodies, she said, "Hi," but did so without looking up. I responded in-kind and both thanked her and asked her what her name was, to which she replied, "Ruby."

A few days later, I ran into our landlord and they let me know that Ruby was having some trouble. She didn't complete her shift the first day because she was scared of being alone, and she told her supervisor that she didn't want to return. I felt bad but told our landlord that we understood completely and would be fine while they found someone else.

To my surprise, a few days later, I ran into Ruby again, this time nearly outside of my office. I asked Ruby how things were going, and this time she looked up at me with a big smile and said things were "very good," and that she was no longer scared. When I asked her what had changed, her eyes lit up and she announced, "All of my friends are here with me," and she pointed to all five of the pieces of artwork that I had collected and displayed in our office. She beamed with pride, telling me the names of each of the artists – which piece Frank did, and Anna did, and Eddie, and so on – that they were watching her work, and this made her feel safe. I bit my lip hard enough to draw blood as I fought back my tears because I knew right then this is why I exist; that if the world stopped tomorrow, I knew I had unwittingly done something that mattered to someone - someone far more important than I'll ever be - if even for just one moment—just like the museum guard had done for me over thirty years ago.

Now that's paying it forward. And that kind of experience cannot be found in a business tutorial or MBA program. It only comes via failure and loss and fear and risk and triumph and a lot of blood and sweat and, yes, tears. Then, and only then, will you know you've made the right decision.

WHAT I *learned*:

- **Diversify constantly.** Never settle for what you have in place currently.

- **Kindness rules.** Give back and pay it forward isn't a cliché, but a way of life.

- **Pay attention to everything around you** as life has a funny way of repeating itself.

- **Next time you hear someone say they simply don't have any extra time, challenge them** to eliminate 25% of what they currently spend time on that they probably shouldn't be.

- **An active imagination is an asset.** Even the skill of pretending will surprisingly come in handy as you ad hoc, hack and hustle your way to success.

two

YOU'RE NEVER GOING TO BE 100% READY

"Fearlessness is like a muscle. I know from my own life that the more I exercise it the more natural it becomes to not let my fears run me."
−Arianna Huffington

've always been restless and probably always will be. I've always been more excited about what's next than what is. And I've always admired explorers and artists, people who seem born to think big, live without boundaries, and who are unapologetic about the risks they take.

So, for me, words and states of being, like *status quo, comfortable, predictable, calculated, perfect,* etc. send me over the edge. They make me feel anything but comfortable. They are the kiss of death to me. And it is not because I'm a cynic and don't believe there's merit, every so often, in feeling comfortable, but those words paint a picture of a person who has given up—who has found a safe place in life and, goshdarnit, isn't going to tempt fate; the kind of person who has normalized complacency and is looking forward to retirement, no matter how many decades away it is.

I suppose I feel this way because my father owned his own business and I spent a lot of time listening to and learning from him. He never stopped thinking, wondering, and talking about work. He was curious about how to improve processes and always seeking ways to make more money, one client at a time.

As I worked my way through a few choice employers, through promotions and raises, I increasingly longed to make my own way as a business owner like my dad and a few other family members of ours. First, I toyed with it. *Do I have what it takes? Can I afford to? When is the right time?* And for a few years, that's where I left things – these amorphous unanswered "hmmm" ponderings. Starting a business was simply an idea of mine, for many years.

Then I tried my hand at real answers, which gave form to addressing the bigger quandary: *What type of business would I own?* For someone who had dabbled at this and that, who still wasn't exceptionally clear on where I excelled or stood out, this was a maddening phase of my discovery (for me and everyone around me). However, I was becoming more and more convinced at this point that I was headed in the right direction.

Yet next came this phase I'll call "The Land of Self-Doubt." Like many of us, I kept finding all the reasons my idea would not work: Why now wasn't the optimal time. Why tomorrow would be better – once I saved a little more money, wrote a business plan, once Madeline was in grade school, etc., etc. There was always a reason to put my dreams off (spoiler alert: there is always a reason, there's a closet full, but only if you keep looking in to find one).

Then it occurred to me that what was really holding me back and missing in my discovery process was knowledge. Cold, hard facts. Why? Because I didn't have any idea what I was embarking upon. Yes, I had this family background and, yes, I had purchased a few *You, Too, Can Own Your Own Business* books and podcasts, but I had never sat face-to-face with someone, especially a woman, and really asked for advice and for their actual experiences.

So, before I sat down with my last employer to walk away from my executive-track position (complete with full benefits and bonuses – so hard to let go of!), I set out to conduct prudent reconnaissance with male and female business owners alike, to see what advice they would give me about starting a business and becoming an entrepreneur. After sipping one too many cups of coffee and glasses of wine, I had acquired my fair share of bruised tales of missing payroll, lame marketing decisions, regretful first hires, high maintenance clients, and far too many examples of bookkeepers gone rogue – essentially the "shoulda, coulda, woulda" business equivalent of what to and what not to do. It was a sobering eye-opener for sure and packed a powerful chaser of reality for this neophyte. I will always be eternally grateful to these amazingly successful entrepreneur warriors – mostly women – who left their battlefield victorious, with pretty fat balance sheets.

Gratitude notwithstanding, it wasn't the kind of advice I *really* needed.

In hindsight, the questions I *didn't know to ask* were the most important ones we should have been discussing. The uncomfortable topics you won't find turning the pages of the newest DIY build-your-own-business bestseller at the airport, or while getting your MBA, or (surprise, surprise) over drinks with badass female entrepreneurs. No one mentioned what I experienced starting out: the loss of friends, the break up of a marriage, the patronizing comments, the loneliness, the uncertainty of decisions and direction, the overall really fucking tough layer of skin you must either have or know how to develop to make this thing called a successful business a reality.

> **No one mentioned what I experienced starting out: the loss of friends, the break up of a marriage, the patronizing comments, the loneliness, the uncertainty of decisions and direction, the overall really fucking tough layer of skin you must either have or know how to develop to make this thing called a successful business a reality.**

No one mentioned these things.

As an optimist, I believe they overlooked these topics because 1) I didn't know to ask those questions and/or 2) because, **as most entrepreneurs do, we willfully and creatively turn all negatives into positives.** We get so good at it that we don't even recall the pain and frustration we once encountered. Selective memory at your service.

But it is not real. And I would be doing a disservice to my fellow tribe members if I didn't share with you what I know to be true. Not that it all will happen to you, or even *any* of it for some of you (if you fall into this micro-minority, you'll need to make some really bad stuff up or no one will like you). Instead, here's my hope for you: **I hope you do experience your own version of some of these obstacles, because for those of you who plan to motivate and inspire your own team or others in your community, without these experiences, you might not have a lot to say. You'll be talking from a place of ego only, lack**ing the punch-in-the-gut perspective of smackdown failure that makes your successful business yours, and yours alone. Your very own messy story - the one you'll speak about to audiences, the one that will be highlighted in articles and nab awards, the one you tell your grandkids about - that's why your customers will choose you. Why your team members will work for you. And why you will be the huge against-all-odds success you already are. Because you are real and brave and want this more than anything, and, most critically, you know what you are getting yourself into emotionally—the stuff they left off the syllabus, textbook, and bar stool.

Now, you must be wondering, *Well, get at it, what kind of business did you end up launching?* There were two things that I heard quite often; two things most successful entrepreneurs would have done differently if they would do it all over again. First, they said they would have narrowed in more closely on what they were best positioned to do well, without a lot of extra work. Meaning, we all have many things we are good at. For me, my areas of expertise ranged between nonprofit fundraising, marketing, public relations, strategic planning, talent, and board leadership. The advice I was given was that's way too many services to begin schlepping around town. As new business owners, we already say *yes* to too many projects we will soon regret, so why cast an even larger net?

Start narrow and build out, if the need and market warrants. This was particularly hard for me as I was working from a place of suppressed fear. Underneath my cool and collected confidence was a woman concerned she was not going to make any money and would have to borrow from some unsuspecting family member (or worse yet, fold and admit failure). So, the idea of limiting what I could say *yes* to was unfathomable.

But I heeded their advice and cut marketing and public relations completely (I didn't have as much experience) and led with what I had the most experience in: fundraising (read: testimonials and cold, hard experience). Soon after came board leadership (because they are so indelibly entwined), and later came strategic planning (because without an overarching organizational strategy, no amount of fancy fundraising is going to fool anyone).

The second thing I often heard was that you cannot do everything. **You must take an immediate cut of your earnings and outsource or hire-in what you are not good at.** Because where you are weak (for me, anything having to do with bookkeeping) will be your demise (I might be using stronger words here, but I certainly took it to heart that way). I was told to read *The E Myth* by Michael E. Gerber, which described why most businesses don't work and essentially says just because you are good at something doesn't mean it will convert into a successful business model. This is a huge myth we like to tell ourselves ("I'm a fabulous fundraiser so, of course, I'll be a fabulous fundraising business owner"), and that explains why a majority of small businesses fail in less than five years. The two are not the same. Hence, my hiring of my aunt to be my bookkeeper. I knew I would excel in sales and service, but not in the stuff that would pay the bills and keep the wheels on the car.

And so, in 2007, the state of Ohio welcomed its newest tax ID# and LLC: *Architectural Philanthropy – building sustainable solutions for nonprofits.*

What the hell was I thinking???

That was one of the worst names in the world. I was trying to be so ridiculously clever it completely backfired on me. Do you know how many people can't spell (nor pronounce) "philanthropy?" Couple that with how many people can't spell "architectural." And that domain name? It was TWENTY-FIVE letters long. A massive flop.

Fortunately, I knew it immediately and figured switching things within six months was far easier than six years later. After the hot mess my first decision created, I decided uncomplicated was cool. Way cool. Even cooler and easy-peasy was using my own God-given name. And signature (yes, it is my actual signature – I've only had three people ask me that in twelve years of business, oddly enough).

And so, in *late* 2007, Aly Sterling Philanthropy was created and kicked Architectural Philanthropy to the curb (official mistake #1 under my belt). The word "philanthropy" still gets a lot of people tongue-tied, but I look at it as a public service. I mean, seriously folks.

WHAT I *learned*:

- Let's face it – just like marriage, children and paying taxes, **you will never be 100% ready to launch.**

- At the same time, **don't plow into a decision without a process, a little strategy and, in my opinion, a big dose of reconnaissance. Take time to ask for advice –** there are so many wonderful people out there willing to give it.

- **Resist the urge to doubt yourself.** If you have to, tie a piece of string around your finger as a reminder.

- **You don't have to be good at everything to be successful.** The most successful of us own our limitations, ask for help, and outsource.

- **Fail and fail often.** Celebrate those failures, because someday you, too, will be writing a book about how important they were.

- **Restless is good.** Don't become complacent. Stay hungry.

three

BE PREPARED TO WATCH OTHERWISE SMART, LOVING, AND USUALLY SUPPORTIVE PEOPLE LOSE THEIR SHIT

"The key to happiness? Don't let anyone rent space in your head for free. That space is prime real estate."
—Alka Dhillon

My first memory of my dad is one of him playing with my sister and me in an indoor pool at a Holiday Inn. I think I was a bit older, even as old as five or six. I'm not sure why I don't have any earlier memories of him, except that he was always working, and my mom or my maternal grandparents were very involved in our lives. In this particular memory, which my sister and I both recall fondly, Dad was chasing us in the pool, yes, pretending to be a shark. We were petrified. Only if you could manage to get out of the pool were you safe. And he was too fast to let that happen.

We spent a lot of time in hotel pools, both indoors and out, as we vacationed a lot. Usually, it wasn't with my dad, but with my mom and her parents—two people who were incredibly kind and loving; two of the nicest people you'll ever meet, and my life is filled with only the best memories of their presence. My grandmother died a few years ago, and my grandfather, who retired at the tender age of ninety, is still alive and loving life at ninety-five (yes, excessive working is in my DNA).

But back to my dad.

My sister and I have only one memory of our paternal grandparents. We visited them as a family when I was probably seven or eight and Annie was three or so. We drove four hours away from northern Ohio to southern Ohio, to a town I had never heard of nor imagined in a fanciful way during my formative years. Because it was far from fancy.

My father was born a hillbilly. He was one of four boys born to Neil and Betty Plants in Philo, Ohio, which is squarely in what is referred to as Appalachia, "a stretch of the eastern United States that includes the Appalachian Mountains, exhibiting long-term poverty and distinctive folkways," according to the New Oxford Dictionary. Poverty was just the tip of the iceberg. Chronic addiction, unemployment, and domestic violence are just a few of the issues plaguing this part of our country. At the same time, hillbillies are also a fiercely loyal and proud people. If you've read J.D. Vance's *Hillbilly Elegy*, you'll know what I'm referring to.

But I didn't understand my father's upbringing. It seemed so different than mine, and my mom talked about it in a way that made me feel like they were straight out of that show *The Beverly Hillbillies.* I truly imagined them as dirty, disheveled, and talking with food in their mouth.

Upon serving in Vietnam, my dad left Philo to move to the big city of Toledo, Ohio to pursue a college degree and a better life. And at the same time, he was disowned by his family. No one left Appalachia without knowing they would never be welcomed back.

But after years of distance, my dad wanted his mother to meet my sister and me. I'm certain he was testing the water to see if there was a chance for reconciliation. After being served squirrel disguised as chicken (and the humor that generated when his mother disclosed the truth, I think with the goal to alienate us), my dad was crushed. This propelled him; it made him even more ambitious and competitive. He had something to prove—his family and upbringing were rooting for him to fail, to ultimately find out that he was no better than they were. Being excommunicated for trying to improve his condition - their condition - brought him sorrow, but did not define him. Proving them wrong became his driving force. Sound familiar?

Moving to Toledo and entering the university wasn't enough for my dad to prove he could make it outside of the holler and without the endorsement of anyone he knew. Upon achieving his two-year degree, he went to work at a locally owned mortgage company and learned all about lending and real estate. I don't remember much of this part of his life, but I did begin to pay attention when he left to go work for a big bank in their mortgage department. There, my dad accelerated his career, climbing the ladder and getting to know many local leaders and real estate agents. There was nothing I liked more than going with him on a weekend, taking a seat at an empty desk, and just taking in everything I saw and overheard. I loved office equipment and office supplies and reading the pink "While You Were Out" notes impaled through that sharp dagger they collected on. I loved the chemical smell of fresh copies (or Xeroxes, or "dittos," as we referred to them), and would steal Bic pens in blue and red for my pencil pouch at school. I was never bored there; the entire scene was thrilling to me (including the behind-the-scenes action I imagined). Everyone seemed so important and like they were doing something consequential.

One night, I overheard my parents talking about my dad's decision to open his own mortgage banking firm with a few financial backers. I was BEAMING. I imagined this meant he would have an entire building like he worked in now, with floors and floors of employees racing around to meet deadlines, papers flying. While it never exactly resembled this notion, the process of opening an office was exhilarating, and I was grateful my dad allowed me to be a small part of it. Even as a pre-teen, I had a strong sense of what being a business owner meant because all my dad talked to me about was work. And he was one helluva hard worker.

My mom, on the other hand, wasn't as thrilled. To this day, I really don't know exactly why, but I do know that shortly after Dad launched his business, my mom asked him for a divorce. And life slid downhill for a few years.

With rare exception, a divorce feels like a tornado for kids—it comes out of nowhere, tears you apart, and turns everything you knew and once believed in upside down. And then, even though you can't believe it's possible at the time, life stabilizes once again. There's a new normal established, new routines and new players in the game, but, in general, life starts back up.

In between the tornado descending and destroying, and the FEMA trailer leaving, it sucked. Suffice it to say, my mother was very upset with my dad and made it her full-time job to be certain everyone knew this, including my sister and me. Because I was older, I managed a pretty good relationship with my dad (he actually served as a refuge from my mom who, again, was just spewing fire most days), but my sister was more vulnerable and felt bad about spending time with our dad since my mom made her feel that way. I think their relationship suffered, permanently in many ways. And I think my mom knew I had a bond with him that even she couldn't break. So, she gave up and moved on to influencing Annie. Ultimately, her attention would turn back to me, as she saw her ex-husband in me, and I would become her nemesis while she figured out her own life.

Life living with my mom was difficult. She wasn't happy, so that meant I wasn't happy. I always felt like she'd take her frustration and her desire to be in control of something out on me. If I was a minute or two late for curfew, I was grounded - for a month. If I asked to go to the grocery store at 10 p.m. at night with my girlfriend to get oranges and popcorn, I was lying. (*What kind of fool did I take her for?*) If I was honest and asked if I could take the car and go to a jazz club half a mile away on a Sunday afternoon, that was an all-ages and had an all-you-can-eat spaghetti bar for three dollars, I was told no – but with a glimmer in her eye. I think she truly *enjoyed* making me upset. I am certain she looked at me and saw my father. And as ridiculous as that was, it made her happy to vicariously hurt him.

Her issues didn't stop me from doing what I wanted to. I just stopped asking permission. And because we shared one car, when I had it, I took it for long stretches of time, and during a time when cell phones didn't exist, it was near impossible to get in touch with me. One fabled Sunday, I did go to Rusty's, the all-ages jazz club, with my friends to enjoy music and endless portions of spaghetti and garlic bread. As my friends and I sat up near the front of the club, right by the stage, my girl-friend leaned over and said, "Hey, I think that's your dad all the way in the back, seated with his girlfriend." And low and behold, it was Dad!

I thought this was the coolest thing ever, and we all went over to say hi and spend some time at their booth. Only after the performance was over and we were walking out would my dad tell me that he'd been *sent there to retrieve me* by my mom, who put two and two together and, lacking a car, coerced my dad to go get me. And retrieve me he did, but first he stayed to take in a great show and visit with me and my friends. I wanted so badly for my mom to know that I really was a good kid and that I would have preferred not to lie to her, but she gave me no choice. After that day, I went to live with my dad.

Feeling judged for things I did not do (or think or feel for that matter) started early for me. I saw my dad judged for leaving his home-town to make a better life for himself. I felt judged for wanting to enjoy my teenage years, keeping my deep-dyed sense of exploration and imag-ination engaged, without the intense scrutiny and controlling reactions of my mom. And soon, the critical (and incorrect) judgment of others I cared so much about – including my spouse - would play out on an even bigger stage with bigger stakes.

If you would have told me twelve years ago that my decision to start my own business would alienate and upset some of my closest friends (and spouse) at that point in time, I would have thought you were being a mean girl. But even during the early stage, when I would subtly tell a few friends what I was *thinking* (I said "thinking" as if it were a random thought that had gingerly crossed my mind, in case they reacted as they actually did), I was dismayed and often deflated by their responses. Although I don't know exactly why, I thought for sure that my peeps would give me a standing O for the idea and concept alone. I did get a little of that, but mostly what I received were raised eyebrows, uncomfortable chatter, or long, drawn-out *Reeeealllys?* of the "You don't say!" variety; as if it was the most foreign thing they'd ever heard. In fairness, however, it was. It had been a part of my upbringing and constantly swirling around *my* consciousness, but entrepreneurship wasn't a part of *their* family upbringing, worldview, or goals.

What quickly became clear was that there were a few different themes in the reactions shared after I initially laid out what I was "thinking" (wink, wink).

One such reaction was to pepper me with many more questions. I welcomed this reaction because I didn't have many answers but now had a growing list of questions, which I needed to figure out answers for quickly. This also showed that, for the most part, these people in my life cared enough to continue to communicate and explore with me. They challenged me in a healthy way, not letting me get too ahead of myself or awash in a deadly dose of passion without enough realism.

The second reaction I experienced came with zero questions and radio silence. These folks were easy to deal with because, well, I didn't have to deal with them anymore. But their opt-out approach left me feeling like I had done something wrong, or that they knew something I didn't.

And the last reaction was the worst. These were the secret society of haters; the ones who acted like they were in my corner, had my back, offered lots of fist pumps and raised glasses, but would then slowly and consistently poke holes in my energy and ideas and momentum, as if it had become their part-time job. Some would applaud my bravery only to ask why my current job and financial success wasn't enough. Others would flatter my vision, but question what I knew about being a business owner. They'd shower me with stats and data that evidenced the uphill (and usually fatal) battle of a start-up. They'd tell me that without a business plan no one would give me the time of day (which was true, even with a business plan). They quietly smiled and snickered when I couldn't get the right words out fast or eloquently enough to describe what I was trying to become. They asked me for proof of concept in such an aggressive way, I worried I was an imposter.

And others would become experts in areas they knew nothing about—those who told me what I wanted to start wasn't a real business. Consultants were akin to traveling medicine shamans. If you can't hack it in the real world, you became a consultant (apply here the age-old stab about teachers). Or how could I make money working with the nonprofit sector? (If I had a nickel for every "'Nonprofit' – *get it,* Aly?" har, har joke…) Or that just because I was good at what I did while working for a major organization did not make me able to do this without backing. And a lot of it.

There was this running punchline (read: my failure) that was most common. It was this notion that my desire to create a nonprofit consulting firm was a temporary fix, until I found a "real" job. I had friends assume it was a way for me to ease out of full-time employment (quite the contrary – I would be working overtime!), and/or assume there wasn't a chance in hell it could work out (thanks for the support, bro). I found myself, once again, drinking a self-doubt cocktail with a dash of anger mixed in. And now it was too late. My shingle was hung. I had to prove these bozos wrong. I had to show them that a woman really can launch just like a man. But it hurt that so many of these bozos were my bozos.

There are a lot of good, really well-intentioned people in your life who do love you and have been there for you forever. But because they see you in the way they are used to seeing you, and used to having you see them, disruptive change (marriage, babies, divorce, leaps off a cliff to start your own business) really rattle them to the core, often because they are scared—not for you, but for them. *What will happen to your relationship? Why hadn't they done something like this yet?* **Every limiting belief that they hold for themselves will be shoved, crammed, and forced upon your decision, like a mirror looking straight back at them.**

Then there are those absolute lovelies, as I passionately refer to them. The people in your life who are so self-aware of their limiting beliefs (usually thanks to years of therapy), so secure with who they are and aren't, and so enthusiastic about the endless opportunities this big amazing universe allows for each and every one of us, that they alone can generate all the love and support you need. More about these rare birds coming up.

As for the others, give them time. They might come around. But in the meantime, it is truly critical that you don't succumb to their negativity, their transposed fears, their subtle but consistent messages of doubt. You must find a way to neutralize them and keep them as far away from your positive vibes and juju as possible.

WHAT I *learned*:

- **Don't take this personally.** It's not about you or your decision. It is about them and their limiting (or untapped) beliefs about themselves.

- **There are people who have been in your life and who have served a purpose thus far along your journey that may not have a function moving forward.** Yeah, it sucks, but time to bless and release.

- **If you keep the non-supporters around, whispering in your ear, causing you to doubt your dreams and decisions, you will not succeed.**

- **Love and hold tight the ones who get your crazy dreams.**

- **Not everyone is going to understand what you are doing.** They most likely aren't hardwired like you are, they lack the visionary and risk-taking kind of mentality you have. As females, we are finally coming into our own and realizing we are capable of anything we set out to do. But this is a new mindset for us—the unraveling of a million years of having submissive to supportive roles—and that simply does not happen overnight.

If you need a reminder of how badass you are, check out the timeline on the next page and remember that you are the product of generations of badass women who fought for your right to independently open your business.

1792

Mary Wollstonecraft publishes
A Vindication of the Rights of Women
(one of the first works of feminist philosophy - but really
just stated the obvious: women are competent and essential)

1820

Women begin to work in factories
(but for far less money than men)

1844

Lowell Female Labor
Reform Association Was Created
(our first attempt at an organized posse, a.k.a. a union)

1869

The Knights of Labor
(our bros demand equal pay across all genders, sexes, and races; organizer
Mother Jones becomes known as "the most dangerous woman in America")

1909

Uprising of the 20,000
(the largest labor strike on record still to this day -
who run the world?)

1918

Women in Industry Service
(as the Great Depression begins, women are relegated
to "female-oriented" jobs, but that doesn't stop us from creating
more dual-income families than ever before)

1943

Rosie the Riveter
(as men go off to war, women take up the
reigns in heavy, male-dominated industries)

JUNE 10, 1963

The Equal Pay Act
(an effort to abolish wage disparity based on sex –
sadly, still a work in progress some 50+ years later)

1964

Civil Rights Act
(aims to end discrimination based on
race, color, religion, sex, or national origin)

1988

Women's Business Ownership Act
(this legislation enabled women to finally be able
to take out business loans - wait for it -
without a male co-signer!)

FEBRUARY 5, 1993

The Family and Medical Leave Act
(you get to keep the get-well-soon card from your boss
AND keep your job when you feel better – how generous!)

MARCH 8, 2017 & 2020

A Day Without Women
(an event organized to emphasize women's importance
in society and to call out economic injustices)

More on this history of women in the workforce:

I love the resurgence of Rosie the Riveter. I am told she was one of the top Halloween costumes last year and her image is finding its way onto candidate campaign materials, collegiate laptop stickers, and experiencing newfound fame being repurposed as a U.S. Postal Service stamp. This reawakening of her iconic image is significant, of course, as she represented the first time women, en masse, went to work to replace men who were drafted to serve in WWII. Today, her image has been appropriated to stand for feminism and women's economic power.

When we think of the arc of humanity and plot the point in time when women began to enter the workforce, compared to present day conditions, yeah, things aren't what they should be, but it's only been a little over sixty years. That's not a long time for the rest of the world to embrace and support this thing called women entrepreneurship. Some people still can't wrap their heads around women working at all, let alone being a CEO or running their own successful business. I'm not trying to create excuses either, but real change demands a generation or two to take hold. In the meantime, we're going to keep flexing our muscles like Rosie.

four

OWN IT: ADMIT YOUR WEAKNESSES EARLY

"You are the average of the five people
you spend the most time with."
–Jim Rohn

People often say, "Wow, you must be so strong, so brave, so confident to start your own business." It would be lazy - misleading, in fact - for me to answer in the affirmative. I would resemble the women I interviewed who were, rightly so, answering my questions in their present moment, sitting across from me strong, brave, and confident. Had I known enough to ask them what they felt like when they launched, or *right before* they launched, my guess is they would answer as I will now: I was anything but strong, brave, and confident. But I was outsized in my optimism, determination, and willingness to work my ass off to become something I knew I could be (soft credit to my father's Appalachian roots).

I slowly generated my own strength and confidence through watching others do it, by listening to their stories and understanding how they thought through things. How they anticipated. How they handled defeat and setbacks. Who were these people? I'm a diehard reader of anything outside of my industry (ranging from any edition of *Fast Company*, a documentary on the Italian chef genius Massimo Bottura, or about how skyscrapers are built, TED talks, books about world leaders, to failed stories of starving artists who only became famous once they died), but I have no shame in asking kindly for advice (followed by a handwritten thank you note) from real people as well.

> **If you want money, ask for advice.**
>
> **If you want advice, ask for money.**

As fundraising professionals, we were always taught that if you want money, ask for advice. If you want advice, ask for money. While I wasn't looking for money, I knew that many successful people are eager to give back and pay things forward. And they also tend to have big egos and love talking about how they got to where they are today and what (or who) they credit their success to (it's a really important question everyone should ponder). So, I listened. And took notes. And listened again. (Ever realize the words "listen" and "silent" contain the exact same letters? Interesting, huh?) I was unusually successful in reaching out to others, men and women alike, none of whom had experience in my industry, to ask them about how they did it, or about their thoughts on an issue I was experiencing, or, without an agenda, just a good reason to connect and catch up and see how they were doing. It is amazing what people will do to help someone out, especially the older they get (and the more time they have or melancholy they become).

But there comes a point when all the advice and conversation in the world isn't enough, or you risk wearing out your welcome (go do something!). At some point, you need to *make shit happen* and show progress to your followers, observers, staff members (or partners and stakeholders, if that's the case). But I needed other people, as there were times in which I was plain stuck and felt like I was looking down the barrel of a shotgun with both eyes closed. I had no idea how to manage bills or invoices. These were not my areas of expertise (I could barely balance my own personal checkbook). And if I were too foolish to pretend I could do it, I would crash and burn. In a pile of unpaid bills. That would make for one lousy tombstone epitaph (and make all those haters right).

Because I did know to check my gut from time to time, I hired a part-time bookkeeper very early on, who was also my aunt (and had experience being a bookkeeper, bonus!). I had heard one too many horror stories of bookkeepers robbing you blind, leading me to believe this was a sound decision. While my profit margins were slimmer, I was in my zone, not out of it. Someone else was handling the things I wasn't good at—the things that would jeopardize my focus and attention as I launched.

Side note: if you hire a family member or friend, here's how to increase your odds of it working out: It's not unusual to consider hiring someone we know to work for us, especially in the beginning. It might be a family member or friend who has been a huge supporter of yours and who has some kind of skill or talent they can offer you and your work. While this can work out nicely, more often than not, it can end up the ruin of an otherwise wonderful relationship. How do you increase the odds of success? Be certain to have the "if this doesn't work out" discussion before the first paycheck is cut. When I hired one of my best friends, Liza, that's exactly what we did. And for a few months, we worked together, but realized for various reasons unrelated to either of us that this might not be the best idea, and *presto*, tore up the paperwork and went back to being friends again. But only because we had a candid conversation first, and both agreed our friendship was most important and would not be placed in jeopardy.

Realizing next that while I loved like crazy the marketing and communications end of our business, if I attempted to fill this need for the firm, I would likewise become distracted. So, I hired a part-time marketing specialist, who was also a full-time mom and friend. She was elated to have a distraction in her life that reminded her daily of her other skills and talents (and she was able to talk to adults instead of toddlers, bonus again!). And so on and so forth. I assembled my team through recognizing my weaknesses and finding flexible and willing talent who would allow me to do what I needed to focus on my vision and expertise.

My recommendation is to surround yourself with people who challenge you, who aren't cut from the same cloth as you are, nor do they have anything to lose by being honest. They'll point out your blind spots and tell you if there is a thirty-foot sinkhole two steps in front of you. They'll question your assumptions and fill your head with seemingly unrelated and crazy ideas that worked for them in completely different industries. Mastering that intersection between what you think you are doing well and what you are completely overlooking is possible through abstract thinking and through embracing (and hoping to avoid again) the hard lessons of failure. I'm all about failing and learning, but if I can minimize my losses a bit by learning vicariously through other business owner's failures, why not?

My go-to collective of people were, and continue to be, a small but mighty group comprised of a yoga studio owner, a financial genius, an attorney, a candy shop owner, and an architect, to name a few. Their only payment has been gratitude and reciprocity. When you start a business, you check your ego at the door and realize that, to be successful, you do not have to have all the answers, **but you do need to seek to find the right questions to ask.** And typically, the best answers and advice will not come from your BFF posse. The best advice will come from people you hire, distant acquaintances and strangers alike, and from hours and hours of late night till-you-pass-out reading about failed dreams and resilient dreamers.

A member of my collective and one of my best friends, Leslie, owns a successful yoga studio called Toledo Yoga, that she started only a few years after I launched Aly Sterling Philanthropy. Leslie went through her own uphill battles at first, beginning with her decision to start with a partner (proceed with caution - more on that specifically to come), to simply entering a saturated market filled with (note the irony here) some pretty cutthroat yoga studio competition (#namastebitches – yes, this is a real thing). In the beginning, and still today, there was nothing I looked more forward to than a late Friday afternoon glass of wine with Leslie after a particularly long and psychologically taxing week. We would compare notes about employee issues, client quirks, family drama, and, always saving the best for last, some knucklehead gender stereotype that was played out on us during the week. It might've been about one of my clients sending an inappropriate text, or about being short or not present with our kids because our heads were everywhere but with them—or wondering how, or better yet, why we wanted this life we'd created. Then we'd make each other feel better and toast to being trailblazers, vulnerable enough to admit flaws and crazy enough to believe we could do it all on our own.

There will be various periods in the growth of your business when you will face decisions that simply overwhelm you. They might happen in isolation, or spaced out nicely throughout a year, or they might unionize and all hit you at once, creating, for me, an overload of issues that made me want curl back up into bed. For a month. These were the moments when I felt most fortunate to be surrounded by my "unofficial" advisory board, who intuitively knew when I felt like I couldn't come up for air and called me out on it, forcing me to talk through things until I had a resolution. They would offer advice - often the kind I would have had to pay a lot of money to a consultant for.

Many of my peers have shied away from forming an official advisory board, worried that they would be inviting in scrutiny and accountability that they would not be able to unwind. Official or unofficial, we need to be held to higher standards and will need to have professional input on the really tough things that are thrown at us. And most importantly, every so often, we need someone to drag our sorry assess out of bed and hand us a big cup of black coffee.

Can we have the partnership conversation real quick? *Where to begin?* I do a lot of mentoring and coaching, happily giving of my time to have conversations with many "contemplating" women considering their launch. The only time I respectfully decline a cup of coffee or glass of wine is when someone is considering a partnership.

First, I don't have that perspective or experience (thankfully), so my sightline is limited. Second, the crash and burn rate is too high. I'm sure there's a massive body of research out there that explains why partnerships aren't as effective and successful as we wish them to be, as I can anecdotally give you one example after the next of the model being flawed. In my opinion, it's akin to a baby blanket – a soft, fuzzy one that makes the fear of the unknown more palatable. *The new venture will be easier if I do it with someone.* Resist this urge, ladies!

Be positive your partner is offering something of real bonafide value, because if not, you could really regret a lot of things in your future. *Like what?* Oh, let's see: Like having to negotiate everything with someone else. Or giving up half of your profits. If those two aren't enough, there's a handful more that will quickly make you wonder *what the $!@# was I thinking?*

WHAT I *learned*:

- **Step out of your ego.** The earlier you are honest about what pieces of your business will be most difficult for you to execute, the better.

- **Inspiration comes from things and people with whom you are not familiar.**

- **Keep your standards high.** If you keep the non-supporters around, whispering in your ear, causing you to doubt your dreams and decision, you will not succeed.

- **Not only do we not have all the answers, often we do not even know what the right questions are!**

- **While adding staff early will cut into your profit, done well, it will yield long-term results and allow you to scale sooner.**

- **You can't see your own blind spots, and neither can your best friends or family** (or they may not be willing to tell you).

- **Gratitude and humility can go a long way.**

five

DON'T RELY ON LUCK:
YOU – AND ONLY YOU – WILL MAKE THIS HAPPEN

"I don't believe in luck. It's persistence, hard work,
and not forgetting your dream."
–Janet Jackson

I have a good friend who loves to debate the concept of luck. He believes there is such a thing, and I don't. Even when I think about the fifty-dollar bill I found on the ground in a grocery store parking lot when I was a teenager, that wasn't luck. That was the intersection of opportunity and action. I saw the bill all crumpled up like a wad of trash (opportunity), and I leaned down and picked it up (action). The notion of luck reminds me of astrology or zodiac signs or mercury in retrograde or tarot cards. As a bachelorette party activity? I'm in. As a way to think of how the world works? Ah, I'll pass.

Opportunity isn't going to take the redline train and show up on your doorstep with a personalized invitation asking you to take action, now will it? It expects you to find it. Create it. Turn over a hundred stones to discover it taking a nap under the very last one. It requires a different kind of vision and perspective, because even the act (or art) of being able to see opportunity takes time. Some of us were born opportunists (a term that has unfairly earned a bad rap and negative connotation), and others of us needed to learn to be, either out of survival or to up our game in a competitive market or because it sounded like a damn better plan than waiting for something to happen.

People think I am an extrovert when they meet me professionally because I am comfortable speaking in public or motivating groups of people to share their innermost personal experiences, but I'm not an extrovert. I'm more of an introvert who loves connectivity, but also has a battery pack that needs recharged. My brand of battery pack recharges through quiet alone time. I love to reflect in silence and find that it is critical to my professional performance. My days are usually outsized: back-to-back meetings, group presentations, sales calls, trying to motivate my kids to do a million things they don't want to do. The idea of then having to do *extra* things—social events, dinner parties, godforsaken home parties (I don't need any more bad jewelry or overpriced skincare, please!)—after 5 p.m. or on the weekend is not the least bit appealing to me.

However, when I look back at some of our firm's most game-changing milestones or moments, almost all were anchored to a situation I reluctantly put myself in, cranky and whining all the way. They usually were the social and charity events I had said yes to months before, and once the date arrived, it was the last thing I wanted to do after working fifteen+ hours that day. Or those volunteer shifts or meetings with community leaders to talk about things that really had nothing to do with my world at that moment in time - until a few months later, they critically did. Or I made a connection with someone who ended up, several months later, being on a review committee for the proposal we just submitted to a nonprofit. The world has a mysterious way of unfolding. One of my dearest friends, Rusty, a magical person everyone should have in their life, has always told me that no one enters our life accidentally. This, I believe, is 100% true.

I know I said I don't believe in luck. However, as a student and devotee of sociology and other social sciences, including psychology, I do give pause and credence to the notion that to whom (and where) we are born can give some of us an upper hand. This is one of the few things in life we can't control. Some of us get lucky, and some of us don't.

But not so fast. There are so many stories of people who are born into impoverished settings, suffer adversity of some sort or the other, and rise. What about my dad who was born in Appalachia? Or [insert your own personal bootstraps hero here]? I was lucky to be born into a fairly intact middleclass family in the heartland of opportunity, the USA. But mine was not a fairytale. There were many things that happened to me that affected me deeply - experiences that made me think I was not good enough nor worthy of positive affection and attention. I was constantly caught in a crossfire of parental animosity, leaving me psychologically abandoned, with only my imagination to depend on.

How we overcome adversity, including the economic variety (extend that to gender and ethnicity as well), is the stuff that case studies and books and documentaries are made of. It's what absolutely inspires and ignites and tells each of us we are The Little Engine That Could.

After all, where there is a will, there is a way, right? Is it always true? No. But it's been a driving force for me – right or wrong. And there's hope in the sentiment that helps us strive to grasp exactly what we deserve.

Defining "will" and "way" is easier said than done. How we show up in the face of criticism, pressure, and adversity is critical to how others define us, and how we allow ourselves to be defined. Let's take the pressure of launching a business for example.

There were many times (then and now) when I didn't know what I was doing. I would schedule a meeting with a prospective client and just hope to God that I didn't ramble, or that when I was asked a question I had a decent answer. How I personally overcame that worry was to ensure that everything I could control about the situation was in place. I had my folder with our information printed on thicker cardstock. I made sure I sent a reminder email a day before, confirming our meeting and indicating how much I was looking forward to it. I did the pre-research and felt familiar with their mission and board (and anything else I could glean online). And I made sure I wore clothing that made me feel confident. When I walked into that room, the first thing they were going to see (before I started talking and potentially ruined it all) was someone who had prepared and looked confident. (P.S. I had maxed my credit card right before my launch, updating my wardrobe to fit my particular industry while not sacrificing my own personal "style" – while the interest rate was high, it was worth every penny).

Right or wrong, we are all judged by how we "show up" to important things, and we all know that judgment takes about a hot second and there's very little opportunity for second chances. Don't allow someone to create an opinion about you because your clothing is more appropriate for a cocktail party than a boardroom [insert your own industry here - clearly, it varies greatly, but you get my point]. Our body language is equally as important as what we wear. How we hold ourselves - are we sitting up straight or slumped? Are we making eye contact or avoiding it? Did we put our phone away or are we monitoring it?

My mother did an excellent job mandating proper posture and etiquette in us from an early age. I hated it then (the painstaking emphasis on where plates should be placed and which fork should be used for which foods, sheesh), but I am grateful now. And how you wore your clothes and held yourself at a table mattered, too. I have vivid memories of my grandmother placing her finger gently in the small of my spine as she passed by me, a not-so-subtle signal that my posture was curved or slumped. I would quickly sit up straight (and roll my eyes), not having any idea of the lasting gift she was giving me.

But your clothing choices and posture alone will not make you successful. There's much more to it, including daily structure and routine and your ability to tune out the noise and chaos around you long enough to make rational and pragmatic decisions. While I thrive on change and disruption (or at least I've been used to it since I was a child—it was the only thing I came to depend on, as messed up as that is), I cannot go more than a few days without the routines and structure I've created in my life. When I'm on the road for more than three days, I become cranky and feel like I'm spinning out of control. All I need is my routine back again - my daily route to work or the drive to pick my kids up at school, my workout, letting my dog out first thing in the morning before I write and brew a pot of coffee - and I feel more balanced and less emotionally wound up.

Just saying, if you think you are busy now, and your life is chaotic and spinning out of control, you will be paralyzed by what's ahead. You need to get your house and your head in order, or you won't be able to stomach the disruption and unpredictability that will define your next few years. There are ways to do this, as I mentioned, through showing up as your very best self, even if internally

> **You have to become even more intentional about routine and structure— the bedrock of this rollercoaster ride.**

you think you are in over your head. You have to become even more intentional about routine and structure—the bedrock of this rollercoaster ride.

One other frequent piece of advice I received during my pre-launch interviews was to develop a code or process by which you can take the emotion out of some of your decision-making, something you will encounter. **The foundation of many successful businesswomen is a core commitment to her values—who she strives to be and how she desires to treat others.** We can say we have certain values, but the process of living them out, I have found, is extremely messy. There's so much grey in our world. It would be far easier to make decisions based on the black and white variety. Rarely is this the case. Usually, I'm bombarded with multiple perspectives, possible outcomes, and political considerations. Like a mad libs book from my youth, there are so many ways the story could end and, often, any of them would be acceptable. You'll find as a business owner this constant push and pull between making decisions that align with your values or blur the boundaries just a little bit because someone is making your life complicated. Take comfort in the fact that we all struggle with this, it's universal, but as long as you continue to try to apply some set of criteria (think *The Four Agreements* or Rotary's Four-Way Test: Is it the truth? Is it fair to all concerned? Will it build goodwill and better friendships? Will it be beneficial to all concerned?), you can avoid a drama here and there.

Last year, our firm decided to put our values and team norms in writing, and to use them to define our culture and apply them as criteria when hiring new team members, rewarding performance for existing members, and deciding when a potential new client was a good fit or not. I cannot tell you how beneficial this has been. We've let go of a team member because she was out of alignment with our values and team norms, and have said no to potential clients (and yes, we do share them with everyone).

Aly Sterling Philanthropy Team Norms:
- We keep our commitments and collective word.
- We come from a place of joy, humor, positivity and gratitude.
- We have an innovative and "can do" mindset.
- Our interactions with others are transparent, kind and intentional.
- We collaborate in a judgment-free zone, speaking and listening with candor and respect.
- We strive to use the best communication method with clearly defined next steps.

So, when someone offers that luck is involved in having a successful business versus a failing one, it's not. It's yet another way people who are jealous or can't muster their own bravery decide to explain away someone else's hard work. **Change your definition of luck to mine: when opportunity meets action. But you must create the opportunities and only you can take the action. No one else will do this for you.** If our goal is to erase the boundaries of what is possible, we must first design an environment that is not always chaotic and out of our control. We must create moments of reflection, routines that center and re-balance us, and a personal and professional image that is value-based, strong, confident, and utterly attractive to others.

WHAT I *learned*:

- **My father would tell me when I was young, there are no lucky breaks.** I think he was right, but there is abundant opportunity just waiting for your amazing self to act upon. You'll need to look for opportunity. It won't come knocking at your door after your crazy fifteen+ hour workday. Go towards the places and people you aren't used to or comfortable around. Create an environment they want to be a part of as well.

- **How we "show up" matters.** You might be having a particularly rough day, but don't let your next possible client know this! Lead with what makes you feel confident, and if it's a new pair of ridiculously expensive shoes, make it happen.

- **Structure will be your best friend.** Create one that works for you.

- **Decide what your personal mantra will be.** Through what lens or values will you make the millions of decisions that come your way, especially the big ones? Not every opportunity that presents itself will be worthy of your action. How will you decide?

JUST WHEN YOU FEEL LIKE FOLDING, DON'T: IF YOU STAY THE COURSE, THE MONEY WILL FOLLOW

"Life begins at the end of your comfort zone."
–Neal Donald Walsh

It was a pivotal day when the Art Academy of Cincinnati came to visit my high school art class. I was sold on them. Though dazzled by my dad's work environment, I believed the life of an artist was for me. Work and the three-piece girl business suit [insert Cake's infamous song here] could wait. I wanted to be part of the counterculture environment. Hell, I was already dating a musician who was fourteen years older than me. And off I was to Cincinnati.

My memories of Cincinnati are fond ones. I loved the hills and architecture and the grit of a bigger city. Routinely, my friends and I would find paintings and art supplies and workshop tools out by the curb of creative people's homes near where we lived, at the top of a big hill called Mt. Adams—people who must have had so much art that they needed to purge. And we were grateful. I loved getting around town (pre-Google Maps), exploring new areas of the city after work or class. I worked nearly full-time while attending school full-time.

Art school proved to be an experience in humility and ego. While I was a fairly decent artist growing up and in high school, I was at the bottom of the paint tube in college. I was routinely blown away by my fellow students' talents, including one of my best friends who also started art school with me. While Julie continued on (and continues today to live out her art), my father rescued me, reminding me that I could continue to be passionate about art on the side, but to consider a less specific bachelor's degree. I agreed with him, finished my year, and moved back to Toledo to live with him and begin back at the University of Toledo.

Coming home to Toledo after Cincinnati was a fairly easy transition as my father allowed me to live a very independent life at his house. First, he worked long hours, and second, he had a girlfriend who lived in Cleveland, so he was routinely gone for the entire weekend. Life back home wasn't too different than life in Cincinnati.

Except that I was bored with school. I grew restless in one major and then changed it for another next quarter. This amounted to many wasted credits, money, and time. Fed up, I decided to take off some time and begin working for my dad, which is when I was *formally* bit by the entrepreneur bug.

I threw myself into work at my dad's company, Plants Mortgage Corporation (PMC), in a way I felt I was born to do. My dad and I would leave the house around the same time in the morning and pretty much enter the driveway at the same time, unless he was headed to one of his favorite bars for a drink after work.

At PMC, I learned about everything. I worked my way up and earned the respect of his team, even some of the most stubborn and paranoid. I started with answering phones, greeting clients, making copies, assembling loan packages to be sent to underwriters for approval decisions. I troubleshooted copy machines, phone systems, early computers, and a first-ever internet and intranet system for employee communication (a prehistoric version of Outlook). I loved being a problem-solver and, *finally*, a useful "Jill of all trades!"

> **To be fair, around the same time, there was another entrepreneurial bug biting me. My Aunt Sue (yes, my future first employee) opened a marvelous candy store at the Erie Street Market called The Sweet Life. I had the honor of creating and hand-painting (art school coming in handy) her logo and signage. Like those little multi-colored candy dots stuck on a long roll of white paper she sold (that never peeled off easily), I was paying attention and inspired by every part of her launch.**

As per my profile, I soon became restless and desired more responsibility and money. I felt I had earned the respect necessary to move up. It was important to me that no one thought my father was giving me an unfair advantage. I even went to the extent of calling him by his first name, Rich, while at work. As I moved into the role of loan processor, I learned about finance – both real estate valuation and the personal finances of all of our customers. It was fascinating to see how much money different professions garnered, and how much debt people had, plus, through having to pull their credit reports, what a credit history was and how it controlled a person's ability to successfully get a mortgage, which leads to home-ownership, which, our country believes, means you are no longer poor. You've made it. And my father had. He not only left his home in Appalachia but he now owned his own, and he could help others to do the same.

My father is a man of very few words. He and I barely spoke, even though we lived in the same house or were driving together to Columbus for some mortgage banking event wherein he was either the president of the board or receiving an award of some type. There were also off-limit things, like what he did in Vietnam or about his upbringing.

Yes, my father was a talented businessman and small business owner, but what really made him stand out and earned him a stellar reputation and customer following was that my dad had a way of calming people down and assuring them things would work out, even when I don't think he always believed the same.

The mortgage industry, as you can imagine, can be frustrating, especially back in the late 1990s. Everything was still written by hand and underwritten by a real human being. It could take sixty days for an approval versus a few hours today. Plus, when you are buying a home or selling one, and something goes wrong, people get pissed. If you find out your loan request is declined, you have now created a domino effect of anger, impacting the seller of the home you thought you were buying and the purchaser of the home you thought you were selling, plus a few other people in the mix. Or people would come in to get a "pre-approval" and find out they had open collections that needed to be paid, or that their income wasn't sufficient to purchase their ideal house. In all, I think about thirty percent of the people we worked with were unhappy at any given time. And as any business owner knows, you do not want any percentage of your client base unhappy, let alone thirty percent.

When I was working the front reception area, it wasn't unusual for me to welcome a couple who wanted nothing to do with my friendliness. They were visibly upset by the news that their loan had been denied and wanted to speak to Rich immediately. I walked quickly back to my dad's office, knocked on the cracked open door, and announced that Mr. and Mrs. Smith were in the waiting room and, *man*, were they pissed off. My dad would set his Waterman fountain pen down and look up at me with a smirk that said, *I've got this. Game on.* And so, I would bring back the Smiths and shut the door behind them.

About thirty minutes later, the Smiths would walk out of his office, pass by my desk and, with wide smiles, thank me for everything. *Presto!* Everything was fine. I would quickly walk back to his office (before he got on the phone again) and beg him to tell me what he said, what they said, and how it all worked out. My dad would calmly tell me all he did was let them vent. They were looking for someone to hear them out and listen. When you did that—when you allowed someone who was frustrated to talk, without interruption—it was often the solution they were looking for. He would remind them that he didn't make the rules, although he wished he did, but that until that day, the following issues in their life would have to be resolved, and then he would give them the tools to do so.

But first and foremost, he didn't judge them, didn't patronize them, didn't make them wrong. He just sat back and let them blow off some steam.

And I'm sure the entire situation was uncomfortable for my dad. It had to be! It's not easy to assuage angry clients calmly and with confidence, but my dad faced this challenge head-on, and that's what helped his business thrive. He leaned into feeling uncomfortable, knowing that the next rung of success was on the other side of those feelings. Working for him helped me see, first-hand, how necessary it is to not shy away from my fear, but to confront it, dissect it, and overcome it. It isn't complacency that keeps us safe—it's emotional risk.

My fears of inadequacy and failure (which, in my bluest moments, meant I would run out of money and make my detractors right) were often quieted or eliminated when I did things that made me uncomfortable. Simple things often. Picking up the phone and calling someone I didn't know well. Going solo to a networking event. Comfortable as the alternative might be, I wasn't going to grow a business sitting behind my desk.

I have a piece of artwork that my daughter and I created together. We glued a silkscreened kitchen towel that I bought at MOCA in LA to a piece of canvas and it says: modern art = I could do that + yeah, but you didn't. It hangs in my office proudly, reminding me how easy it is to think about doing something or to talk about doing something, but to truly DO something is not as easy as it looks. It's damn hard—the kind of hard that dumps you in a complete space of uncertainty. No playbook, no rules, no guardrails. Just a key to an unmarked car located in a garage the size of Texas. May the force be with you.

Like the piece of art: entrepreneur = hard + lonely. No one tells you exactly how lonely starting your own business can be. One of my best friends and partner-in-crime, Jen, who was about a year into her start-up, shared with me how much she longed for the days of performance evaluations—those bygone years when her supervisor was awkwardly mandated to meet with her and tell her how she was doing against what was expected of her. "Today, I don't even know what's expected of me. I feel like I'm making this stuff up!" she nervously laughed. But her nostalgia was real. She missed receiving any kind of feedback at all—someone to tell her what she should try differently and what her next goal set might be. Not enough to rewind and go back, mind you, but enough to have been sorry for taking the formality surrounding it for granted all those years.

As entrepreneurs, we learn to benchmark in whatever way we can—seeking out companies who are like yours, either within your industry or by size and scale, or through someone you know who is willing to share. I was fortunate that there exists an international association of nonprofit consulting firms, and once I qualified to apply as a member, I did. And it has paid back in spades by just being around people more senior and experienced than me, and hearing about all the things they've done to create their wins and their losses. Unless you are buying into a franchise, finding a network or organization by which to benchmark can take a lot of time and money. But it's worth the chase.

If you are cut from the cloth of predictability, structure, and clarity around norms and expectations, being an entrepreneur is most likely not a good fit for you (unless you have a great coach or partner). As I mentioned previously, you can take as many classes, read as many books, and talk to as many experts on business planning as you have time for, but, in the end, it is messy, dirty, and unscripted. But if you were the kind of kid I was – who was never very good at one particular thing, but instead a grazer – sampling a little of everything that was going on in the world, you'll find that to be a very useful trait. *Finally, oh, finally!* I was able to realize a benefit from being so-so at everything, from being a connoisseur of life and do-overs and not reading directions very well. Take that, all you child prodigy pianists! And you, body-twisting gymnasts! And National Honor Society valedictorians! How is that working for you now? (My Catholic guilt just took a ruler and hit me across my knuckles and so I offer that I didn't really seriously mean that last statement, of course.)

> **I was a run-of-the-mill, solid B student. I was holding up the middle, let's just say. Five years ago, my high school asked me to give the keynote for the National Honor Society assembly! Life does come full circle.**

As a kid, I so badly wanted to stand out and have my parents brag about how awesome I was at playing the piano ("No one in our family ever played an instrument. I don't know where her talent comes from!"), or that I had mastered a second language ("It was hard to choose between Latin or Mandarin, but I think she made the right decision!"), or that I was going to state playoffs for tennis ("I knew her height would come in handy someday!"). I longed to be someone who could impress at Christmas dinners and family reunions. I wanted to be that child who when I heard my mom talking to her third cousin, twice removed in Chicago, she would be bragging about my achievements and accolades. In reality, the best I pulled off was winning the "biggest bubble" Hubba Bubba contest at the local mall when I was in fifth grade.

Once I broke up with Jonathan (to be fair, I don't think I ever broke up with him, his residual is still alive today), moving further into the real world and smack dab into middle school, all I wanted was to be fabulously spectacular at something. And if it was something that no one else knew how to do, all the better.

There were many failed attempts to be something special; to be as good as that kid I read about in the *Highlights* magazine who could solve the Rubik's Cube in less than ninety seconds. Or the home-schooled girl with braces I saw on the news who was getting into Princeton at sixteen. Or the local teen who somehow made it into the current Sears catalog, wearing the newest ugly plaid sweater dress for fall. *How was she discovered? How could I stand out in that same way?*

But I did stand out, just not in the way I had been dreaming about. There's something very important that you need to know about me during my childhood and into young adulthood, something that ended up drawing attention to me in a way I did not desire, and that is my height and weight. I was the tallest person in my grade, far taller than any girl or boy. I wore a size nine shoe and I was a string bean. If I even looked at food, I burned calories. This got me "discovered" by my school nurse, gym teacher, and music teacher, but alas, it did not, however, get me discovered by boys. I was usually picked on by them (knowing now it was because they worried their post-puberty height probably wouldn't reach mine).

Nurse Mary routinely pulled me out of line to question me about my eating habits. She'd perform a quick scoliosis test while pulling back the tab of a can of Ensure, requiring me to guzzle down this horrible chalky-tasting weight gain supplement. Nurse Mary would ask me to detail what I ate for breakfast, inspect my lunch, and strongly recommend that I had protein for dinner. Next up, aggressive questions about what I did with my food. Did I actually eat it? Did I throw it away or, worse yet, throw it up? No matter what I said, she didn't believe me. Hell, I didn't even know people threw up food at that point in my life. When I returned to class or the lunchroom or the line I had been yanked from, the looks I received from my classmates were painful. I'm sure the roots of my "I'm not good enough" limiting belief, passed down in the genes of my father, were cemented during those years.

If I could go back in time, I would have figured out how to play basketball, because if the number of times I was asked if I played is an indicator, I missed one hell of an opportunity. I couldn't shake my gym teacher from her incessant pleading and quips that "I was wasting my God-given height advantage" (and at a Catholic school, at a minimum, that demands confession).

Finally, the worst upon worst junior high tragedies, for which my height can be blamed, was committed by my music teacher, who also doubled as our director for all school plays and musicals. Mrs. Zimmerman (a.k.a. Mrs. Z) was planning our annual Christmas school recital and needed an angel to sing the concluding song for the evening. The angel was to stand above baby Jesus, Mary and Joseph, and belt out *O Holy Night*. And she asked ME! I was over-the-moon excited and ready to debut.

As our afterschool practices crept closer to performance night, I worried that Mrs. Z wasn't happy with the way I sang. I knew I didn't have a good singing voice (or speaking voice, for that matter), and I wondered why she gave me the role without an audition. About a week before our performance, Mrs. Z asked if she could speak to me after school, I learned the truth: I was selected because of my height. They wouldn't need to invest in a "lift" of any kind if I was cast as the angel. To add insult to injury, she continued to inform me that my vocals just weren't going to cut it, so I would need to LIP SYNC the songs and she would have another student sing them. I was mortified. *How was that going to work?* I knew Milli Vanilli could get away with such things, but I'm no professional lip syncer! Knowing how awkward it would be to back out (as if my parents would let me), I whined all the way to the recital and then waited quietly behind the curtain till it was my turn to take the stage and put an end to another long and miserable grade school Christmas concert. With dry ice blowing around me (and up my flammable polyester robe), I hovered over two shitty kids from a grade above mine, a fake baby, and lip-synced the words to *O Holy Night*.

Here's another kicker. Mrs. Z – who was old enough to have her own kids in college – sang! There wasn't a chance anyone thought that voice was mine. I made my parents bolt home as I didn't know what to say if someone had actually congratulated me. The entire memory, while horrific then, makes people laugh today, including me. I'm reminded of it each time I'm asked at the grocery store to help someone with an item on a high shelf. Height is a wonderful thing.

My mother also believed that my height and weight, and in her opinion, my youth and beauty, would play out well in modeling. This was the one way that my mom did put pressure on me to perform or stand out. A model herself, both when she was in high school and college, and also still as an adult, she would be asked to partake in fashion shows at the mall or a department store. My mom loved fashion, but she really loved modeling and I know wished she had done more of it and on a bigger scale. For about two years when I was in seventh and eighth grade, I went with my mom to NYC and we would literally pound the pavement. She would have looked up several national and international modeling houses and we would just show up, often unannounced and without an appointment. God love her, she was certain they would make an exception for me. I had my portfolio with me (yes, indeed, she made me work with a photographer to assemble a loose grouping of photos—me in awkward poses with bold eighties clothing and way too much makeup). Trot me out, she would, fawning over me, embarrassing me, but I knew *every single minute* of it made her happy. She was in her element, her city, and damnit, wasn't going to let the opportunity that she had missed pass me by, too.

But pass me by, it did. Alas, I wasn't print or runway material.

Shocker.

The experience itself was useful. Asking a stranger to assess you – the outward you – and then give feedback as to why you didn't measure up is incredibly raw. Critique after critique made me almost immune to what they were saying by the end, and, thankfully, I didn't take any of it personally. I'm certain my mom was the only one who shed tears (but she did get some great shopping in).

Knowing my future would not include a stage or runway, I took aim and latched on to elevating my "stand out" status through being hip to trends. A prime example was if you were born in the early to mid-seventies, you grew up during a time when collecting stickers was the biggest thing ever. My friends and I collected all types of stickers – puffy ones, scratch-and-sniff, Hello Kitty, you name it – and we carefully placed them in an old school photo album, perfectly ordered and categorized, so we could trade them with one another at recess or after school. I would get ridiculously jealous of some of my friends who had way more stickers than I did, and my mom refused to continue buying them for me, citing the fact this fad would soon die.

One day in second grade, I was left in my homeroom after school and spied an open pack of delicious popcorn scratch-and-sniff stickers minding their own business on my teacher's desk. None of my friends had these stickers yet and I would be a rockstar if I managed to have them before anyone else. You know how this story plays out, don't you? Indeed, I stole them off her desk. When I was called to the janitor's closet to meet with my (female, thankfully, but still weird place to meet) teacher two days later, she had already alerted my parents, but did not inform the school. I was given another opportunity to redeem myself. From that point forward, I realized breaking the moral laws of my Catholic grade school was probably not the way I wanted to stand out. Nor was this the kind of attention I was seeking from my mother.

No matter the state of my angst or restlessness, throughout my childhood, I was collecting so many valuable experiences. I had slowly evolved into an opportunity junkie, seeking new people, activities, knowledge, and more. Yet I was crushingly hard on myself for not standing out, not realizing these early decades of my life would serve me far better than having some narrow focus or talent.

It's pretty messed up when you are given a relaxed atmosphere as a child and it bothers you; when trips to the mall and nights eating popcorn and watching *Magnum P.I.* and *The Love Boat* are unfulfilling—when you begin to envy parents who I knew pushed their kids to the brink and made them complete jerks—so you create your own universe. I saw my parents' ambivalence as single-handedly limiting my life potential. I was left with only me to motivate, well, me. In hindsight, wow, what a gift that was. I didn't need anyone else to define or determine my happiness or my fate. I could do that all by myself. **As I grew up, I felt comfortable taking the risks others were afraid of. I thrived in dicey situations, diplomatically found my way out of trouble, and could smell and smooth over conflict before it even erupted.**

But we don't have to risk everything or be in a state uncomfortableness 24/7. Actually, most entrepreneurs are quite risk averse, *which is something that makes us stand out from the pack.* Most of our moves are calculated and strategic despite a myth that we are renegades. When I started the firm, I negotiated with my employer, who let me work part-time for a full year while I launched. In turn, I did the same for one of my employees who wanted to launch her own wellness and nutrition business but was concerned about leaving the safety of a salary. A common theme! **There are so many ways to create a personal safety net alongside doing something that is a bit risky and a way bit uncomfortable.**

And in the beginning, even though your emotions will try to get the best of you and tempt you back into the comfort of full-time employment, **STAND YOUR GROUND AND STAY THE COURSE!** Like any other difficult change we make in life, the first part is the hardest. Our brains want to retreat, reject the new normal, and say hello again to [insert your own temptation or addiction or rut here]. Staying the course is essential to financial success. Creating a business plan, no matter how simple it is, and monitoring it often, going back to it when things feel amiss, will become your best friend. You'll have to say yes to things in the beginning that you might not say yes to after a few years. You'll need work and cash flow and a growing client list to leverage and talk about to others. So, don't beat yourself up for taking on a few lousy clients or projects at first. We've all been there. Just know you are doing it for a reason and learn from it (and don't forget who they are when they come back several years later in a one-hundred percent unchanged state and you get to refer them to your competitors).

The world is full of opportunity, and unless you are in an industry just overflowing with suppliers and very little demand, my guess is you've picked something to specialize in that will allow you to ultimately be choosy, someday. Take this time to get uncomfortable, make some mistakes and hustle. It's the only way you'll figure out what you don't want to compromise on later.

Staying the course will pay off. And very often, in a monetary way. While it might take time, even a few years to break even or profit, it will feel so good. Building credibility and trust and reputation is the currency that converts to real money. Nothing else does – everything else is a shortcut or work-around and cannot be sustained. While it is okay to take on a few subpar clients, or start your rates lower than you'd like, be sure not to mess

> **Building credibility and trust and reputation is the currency that converts to real money.**

around with credibility and reputation. Make good on your word, even if it means walking away and leaving money on the table. And resist the urge to drift too far away from your core service or business model. Chasing opportunities is one thing, chasing the wrong ones that create doubt or confusion in the marketplace is another. You are building a brand and a reputation – something that, done right, will generate years of revenue and equity.

Speaking of equity, after our firm turned ten years old, I had a fairly surreal experience of having the option of being acquired by a private equity firm. Hell, I had to look up what that even meant! I quickly surrounded myself with those much smarter than me (remember that financial genius in chapter four?) and embarked on exploring the offer. Never have I felt like my financials were so up for debate. It was a forensic undertaking and I was grateful to those who helped me learn – in an intense way – how the world of private equity works. While we were, and still are, a small firm, our suitors were attracted to our brand and reputation (which also happens to be me and my name), and saw a strong upside to acquiring us in order to attract more "vertical" markets (read: those kinds of companies who are non-competitive but complementary).

While the offer was both flattering and lucrative, I ultimately said no. I am not ready to give over my brand and watch it be drastically altered (and never be mine again). What I did soak in like a sponge was how they would "optimize" our firm once they took over – performance and process improvements that would extract more profit and increase productivity. It showed me what I've not done enough of over the years and lit a new fire under me to do the same – not in the extreme way they would have, but in a way that did improve our bottom line, for our team and for me.

So, just when you feel like folding, don't. You are close, so close that it's imperceptible to the untrained eye, but soon you'll look back and know exactly the day you arrived.

WHAT I *learned:*

- There's a myth that stands in the way of women saying yes to launching – it's that you have to go cold turkey and quit your day job. That's not true. Some of the most successful entrepreneurs I know were strategic and kept both for a while. Including me.

- **Think more like an opportunist in the beginning.** Say yes to more things, be creative with partnerships, make more mistakes. Cash flow is a bitch, so you'll hustle more and take on projects and clients that you probably shouldn't, knowing this will not be the way you'll operate later.

- **Come from a place of plenty versus scarcity.** Or in the powerful words that Earl Nightingale wrote in 1950: "We become what we think about most of the time, and that's the strangest secret."

seven

NEVER, EVER APOLOGIZE FOR BEING AMBITIOUS

"If your dreams do not scare you, they are not big enough."
–Ellen Johnson Sirleaf

I was raised by my divorced, work-obsessed (read: not going back to Appalachia) father through my young adult years, which left me normalizing many things I potentially shouldn't have. The number of hours my father worked was epic. Nonstop really. He was gone by the time I woke up, and often not home till late evening. He worked on weekends. He worked while eating and driving (he was one of the first people to have the first version of a cell phone - a "bag" phone - remember those? They were a forerunner to the flip phone. It was a full-sized phone, Velcro-encased and tethered to a massive cord that you forcefully shoved into the car lighter. There was nothing discrete about it, and people thought you were from Mars talking on a phone IN YOUR CAR). And if I am to guess, like me, he worked while sleeping. (Yes, this is possible—I can put a thought or issue in my mind before I go to sleep and very often wake up with a new perspective or solution. I've also nearly purchased a roundtrip airline ticket to San Francisco on my Delta app while sleeping, so there's the downside.)

Once in a great while, my dad would come home early, pour himself a healthy glass of whiskey, and disappear into an oversized leather chair. He would recline back and drift off after reading the newspaper or work documents. There were nights I would find him there when I got home from being out at the clubs with my friends or, if it was a weekend, when I was up early to leave for a job, he was still there, snoring. (Side note: Indeed, one job when I was in college wasn't enough. I typically held two or three for various reasons, mostly having to do with extra money, but also variety. I loved different environments and the people who came with them, from video stores to an art museum gift shop to selling cosmetics at a department store.) I just assumed everyone worked like a crazy person.

Once I was married - really feeling like I was *adulting* - and for the first time living with a man other than my father, I expected to find that everyone else also operates like my dad (and me). I came to realize this isn't true. I found most people did not work at the frenzied pace he (and now I) did. In fact, most people appeared to have a lot of discretionary time to do things they enjoyed. Hobbies and exercise and television. I felt like work was my hobby. For me, I didn't take to gardening or scrapbooking, but to dreaming and planning and writing down ways to create new or better ways to work or create revenue. As you can imagine, I was a helluva lot of fun at parties.

As a newlywed, in between finishing my undergrad, my graduate degree, working full-time, and being pregnant with Madeline, I would babysit my in-laws' younger children, staying at their house while they vacationed, and teaching art classes to their fourth-grade friends. We would take field trips to cemeteries and farms and draw what we saw and imagined. My every hour was filled.

Sitting in my graduate sociology class, a rousing class on sexual deviance, a fellow grad student turned to me and whispered, "When is your due date?" A fair question given I was over eight months pregnant, my basketball belly being the focal point of my body, constantly throwing me off balance. I replied, "Tomorrow, at 10 a.m."

That's how I rolled with baby number one, two, and three. All scheduled inductions, because I could. My OB said it was safe and perfect for a "workaholic" like me. And it was. I was working more than forty hours a week, taking a full load of graduate classes, and pregnant with Madeline, my first daughter. I remember my esteemed sociology professor (a man who also ran a medical device company, as well as being a tenured college professor with a very impressive record in both) asking how long I would be taking off. Insert bewilderment. This was the first time it occurred to me that I wouldn't be able to show up for class the following day. I knew I would be taking off my paid work, as I was forced to plan that out a few months prior, but I hadn't considered all my extracurricular activities (most consequential, graduate school). I told my professor I would be in touch later in the week to let him know. As it turned out, I felt fine to return to my night classes in about a week. Leaving Madeline in the good care of her father, I grabbed the car keys and zoomed back to the university.

I remember that first car drive vividly. I felt superhuman. It was akin to an out-of-body experience. I was a mom, something I wasn't the last time I was driving a car to class. I was a new me. I had a new distinction, new responsibility, and a new perspective on life. Someone needed me in a way I had not prepared for—in a primal I-*literally*-can't-live-without-you sort of way. I was conscious of this, and embraced whatever it meant, but, most importantly, I was fueled, really revved up to take on the world with a kind of energy and determination I hadn't experienced before. Giving birth and becoming a mother made me ambitious.

With Amelia, my second daughter, also a scheduled delivery, I was working from home within no time, and when she was six weeks old, the newest Sterling infant had been dropped off at our wonderful Danish caregiver's home to join her older sister, Madeline. Fast forward four and a half years later, their youngest sibling, Gabi, would also arrive on time and on schedule to complete a trio of daughters.

When I was pregnant with Gabi, I worked for a regional health-care system, and my office was on the bottom floor of the hospital. Everyone joked that that I might sneak away, announcing I was going to lunch, and actually give birth instead on the maternity floor. Because of this, I was encouraged to schedule Gabi's birth at another one of their hospitals a few miles away. In retrospect, it was an excellent decision. God knows I might have popped her out, cleaned up, borrowed a wheelchair, and spun back to my office to finish my paperwork.

Culturally, it feels like we have come to accept this kind of planning and determination (and admittedly, often insane preoccupation with resuming life and getting back to work) from our male counterparts. But when I embraced it, it didn't go over so well with others. "It's just a job, it will still be there when you get back," I heard often. **But it wasn't just a job. It was a career trajectory. It was the other half of a desperately needed dual income, and, most importantly, it was an insurance policy for my future,** guaranteeing, I hoped, that I wouldn't end up like others around me, nearing retirement broke and without options.

When the internet was young, I was buying up domain names for my girls and for business ideas I was hoping to bring to life. My dear friend from high school had moved to Morocco to begin a kid's clothing and décor business in the Berber countryside where her husband had been raised (where labor was skilled and brilliant vegetable-based dyes were plenty). Julie asked me if I wanted to run their shipping distribution and PR campaign in America. "Why not?" I answered. *Bring it on!* Late in the evening, when Madeline and then Amelia were asleep, I was online, researching media outlets in NYC and LA and reaching out to them with newly created press releases (I would also end up with shipping containers of their products in my garage, much to the chagrin of my husband as he chipped the freezing snow off his windshield in the morning because our cars wouldn't fit in the garage any longer).

After my last daughter was born, I knew I had to channel this ambition and energy differently. I knew that instead of helping grow other people's businesses, I would start my own, but I struggled with deciding what it would be. I had done so many varied things, often not terribly well, but I gained so much experience. There were so many possibilities! It was paralyzing at times, and, I know, highly annoying to those closest to me. I took to writing down business ideas. I thought by putting things on paper I would be able to discern more easily which would be best to pursue. I can remember sitting at a roller-skating party for Madeline, all the other moms (and some dads) socializing while they watched their kids skate, and I sat there, in one of those hard, smooth, curved booths (undoubtedly original from the 1970s), with my laptop, pecking away business plans. *Would it be a marketing firm? A fundraising firm?* Or, at one point, I really wanted to start a pre-teen nail and skincare franchise (called PrairieBlue—had the whole thing detailed down to the fact that I would need to get my cosmetology license). I think that last one put my poor husband, Stephen, over the edge. I knew by his response that would be the last idea I shared with him until I knew I had a final one. And even then, I was too late.

When you have so many ideas, it can become paralyzing. For the sake of your sanity, and those around you (and because the clock is ticking), a rational person knows when they need to pick one thing and commit to it. I suspect many develop a spreadsheet for such decisions, carefully calculating risk and reward scenarios. For me, I needed divine intervention. Read on.

Over the span of a few weeks during the summer of 2006, I found myself on a return flight, sitting right behind two Grey Nuns. I studied how they spoke and interacted with each other, so thoughtful and considerate, as if every single word was full of intention and grace. "Would you please pull the window shut, Jane?" Then, with a small flick of her covered wrist, the window blind was closed, and they put their heads back and dozed off. I watched them, thinking how nice it would be to not have a million ideas racing through my head. To just turn off. To speak slowly. Inspired by their simplicity (or at least the storyline I was giving them—for all I know, they were plagued with anxiety), I made the decision, right then and there, with Sister Jane (I didn't catch the name of her friend) as my witness, to reduce my business ideas to two: a nonprofit marketing firm or a fundraising firm. Thank you slow-moving, slow-talking, and mind-blowingly tranquilizing Grey Nuns.

I spent the next two weeks really evaluating the pros and cons of my two manageable business ideas. It was amazing once I narrowed the playing field how easy it was to focus and really put myself in each (very similar) situation. I considered the upstart needs, ease of entry, resources, and positioning. Had it been necessary to carry all those ideas in my head (and on paper) for as long as I did? I'm not sure to this day. I often tell others who are considering multiple options for their businesses that as long as they are self-aware and in tune with their environment, the universe (or your frustrated friends and spouses) will keep you in check. There will come a point when it will be so obvious, or you'll just become so fed up with the burden of feeding so many ideas and thoughts, that you'll put yourself out of your own misery.

My second nun encounter, the one that solidified things completely, was strange because the nun was more an apparition who showed up during a solo walk in the woods one gorgeous fall day. Over several months, as I was searching and sifting through ideas, I had taken to long walks along either a paved bike path near our house or driving to one of a few parks that I had become particularly fond of because of how lost I could become in the quiet simplicity of trees. (The bike path was along

multiple neighborhoods, and I am too easily distracted by watching people interact, evaluating how people outfit their backyards, or wondering
why I, too, had chosen a subdivision where everyone's homes look exactly alike. *What did that say about the life I had chosen and was soon to extract
myself from?* I digress.)

It was particularly quiet during this walk. I probably passed two
or three people for the entire four-mile loop. The air was chilly and crisp
and, because it was colder, I could hear the rustle of the leaves as I walked
my usual fast pace. The sky was blue and vast. Around halfway through, I
was revisiting a conversation I'd had a year or so earlier with a Franciscan
nun I served alongside on a professional fundraising committee. Sister
Carol Ann Grace complimented my style, work ethic, and dedication to
the nonprofit sector and pursuit of improving the art and science of fundraising, which is something not many see as their calling. Most aren't any
good at it and, in general, it ranks right below public speaking as something human civilization avoids. *Eureka! My "walk in the park" epiphany.*
All this meant there is a definite marketplace for what I'm selling. As I re-
called this conversation and reflected upon it on my flight home, coupled
with my observation of the Grey Nuns and their calm and dedication, I
decided these two experiences and three nuns equaled my future. A nonprofit fundraising firm it would be.

Ambition is a gift. It's necessary and intoxicating and often a
burden. It never leaves me, even in my most quiet moments, and when
I wake up it is there, waiting for me, ensuring my past is not my future. This obsession manifests through thoughts of how something that
exists could be improved. That could include a service my firm offers,

or a marketing campaign I came across in a magazine, or how signage and wayfinding in hospitals and major airports could be more intuitive. I've told a few friends that I would drop everything today if I could be a modern version of a secret shopper. I would love to spend my days visiting hotels, restaurants, retail stores, and hospitals – any place that interacts with and profits from the general public – and offer advice on what they are currently doing well and what they are

> **Ambition is a gift. It's necessary and intoxicating and often a burden. It never leaves me, even in my most quiet moments, and when I wake up it is there, waiting for me, ensuring my past is not my future.**

completely whiffing on. My ambition also manifests through thoughts of new services, new ventures, *new, new, new. What is right around the corner of our industry that I need to know now?* My biggest fear is not just being obsolete, but having a competitor get to a new and significant industry change first.

And so, I obsess. I take in everything around me, I listen, I run scenarios in my head. I'm a walking *what-if?* or, more often, *what's-possible?* I've learned to regulate how I share this with others as it can be an almost hyper-energy that, while thrilling to me, can be draining to others. I've gotten better at not burdening my team with every idea, rather I only bring them the ones that I think deserve further vetting, which might be two to three a year. While my friends have always been fairly tolerant (and partially amused), Stephen was not. Stephen had to endure a lot of dreaming and discussions about the *what-if-?* and *what's-possible-?* which, for whatever reason, didn't appeal to him. I would be playing armchair therapist if I wagered a guess, so I won't. Let's leave it at having me around, pre-launch, was a lot to handle.

WHAT I *learned*:

- Ambition is essential and will manifest itself in each fiber of your being if you let it.

- If you feel compelled to apologize for being ambitious, stop. There is nothing to be sorry about. Most people wish they were more ambitious.

- Invite in all the thoughts and ideas you have about your business, no matter how random or incongruent they are. They won't stay there forever, and you'll find a way to curate them into a manageable few, and then the ideal one.

- Look for inspiration everywhere and in everything: on a plane, in the woods, in people who enter your life in possibly serendipitous ways.

eight

THERE'S NO SUCH THING AS PERFECT TIMING

"If you obey all the rules, you miss all the fun."
–Katharine Hepburn

I was married, just entered my graduate program, and pregnant when my father told me that I needed to go work somewhere else. I was stunned. *Was I not performing well?* Once I calmed down, my father explained that he wanted me to experience work in a different setting, to put my degree and soon-to-be-graduate degree to use elsewhere so that I could be sure I truly wanted to continue to work for him and, ultimately, take over his business. This seemed like such a radical thing to do – to let someone go and put their best interests first. In my company today, we live this practice, but at twenty-two, I had never experienced this concept. Once again, my father showing unconditional acceptance. I agreed with him and was excited about what I believed would be a temporary leave of absence. But in the end, I would never go back.

First, I spent time at an HIV/AIDS service organization called David's House, which was every bit like a small business—stressful, chaotic, and trying my hardest to raise enough money to pay the light bill, while also courting major gifts from big donors, not letting them know how precarious our situation was. This is where I was bit by the nonprofit bug. *Could I apply my business acumen within an industry I was truly passionate about?* They seemed to need me, to need my skillset. Truth be told, I wasn't really passionate about the mortgage industry. I just loved working that hard and alongside my father.

The chaos that was David's House seeped into my personal life and I had a miscarriage. Stephen and I mourned the loss of our never-to-be-met son or daughter, and took comfort in believing that the baby wasn't meant to be for various reasons, that our bodies are incredibly perceptive, knowing when it's not going to be a good fit—a bit of foreshadowing for certain, as I believe my body told me two more important things over the next decade and a half: when to begin as an entrepreneur and when I needed to leave my husband.

After the rollercoaster that was David's House, my professional path became a little less bumpy. My mother-in-law was serving on the board of a regional mental health provider called Harbor Behavioral Healthcare. The executive director position of their foundation was open, and it was definitely a step up from where I was. This would be new territory for me. While I was slightly familiar with fundraising, the kind I practiced at David's House was akin to guerrilla warfare. This new opportunity felt sophisticated.

Before my interview, I crammed like it was the day before a big exam to ensure I was updated on all that was happening in the foundation fundraising space. I took out books from the library, read journal upon journal, and pretty much, for one day at least, was an expert in my field. I landed the job after several interviews and fell further in love with non-profits.

While working at Harbor, we welcomed our second daughter, Amelia. She, like many other children, was conceived pretty much after 9/11 in an attempt to make something better and have control over a world that felt spinning away from us. In five years with Harbor, I took on many positions and held increasing responsibility. It was thrilling and I loved the variety and pace. Here is where I first considered leaving to start my business, but am glad Stephen reminded me that I had not conducted a capital campaign, which was an important milestone to achieve if my business had anything to do with nonprofit fundraising, which I figured it would.

My next and final employer, ProMedica Health System, was, and is, a formidable healthcare system nationally. There, I honed my craft. I dodged bullets, learned how to see invisible landmines and, overall, appreciate effective strategy on a comprehensive and multi-level scale. It is also where I would be inspired by my donors in a way that would motivate me to want to help nonprofits - of *all* shapes and sizes - be effective and attractive enough to warrant the same caliber of success.

Finally, I realized I had narrowed my "Jill of all trades" resume and found a more focused talent that was at once enjoyable, valuable, and marketable.

Over the next four years, I learned more and dreamt more, struggling to define exactly what facet of the nonprofit business model I wanted to occupy. Stephen and I also began to drift. He would drift towards current events and politics. I would drift towards business planning and my next chapter. Our worlds would never again collide in a happy or synergistic way.

We went on trips that he'd won as a result of his growing financial franchise, a local outpost of a national financial advising firm. He worked hard to pass his tests and start his own office, knocking on doors and endlessly following up with prospects until they opened or transferred accounts. I was impressed with his constant motivation through Madeline and Amelia's births. And while I made a decent but fixed salary, he saw a wider range of benefits as a result of his efforts—bonuses, better offices, bi-annual trips to beautiful places we could choose from.

I had a growing feeling I didn't fit into his work scene. We would spend time with his fellow brokers and their spouses, whether it be at regional dinners and awards banquets or alongside them by the pool when we picked matching vacations out of a catalogue. I didn't understand who Stephen had become. He talked about economics and politics and socio-economic issues, but not in an inclusive way, rather in a way that made me feel like an elitist—like I was slowly, but surely, being converted into a club that my people - artists, intellectuals, the marginalized of the world - were not allowed to join. I felt like an outsider. When I was younger and pushed into any mainstream lane, I bucked and bucked hard. I thought this was what Stephen liked about me? I talked about disrupters, about the impact of excess upon the struggling classes, about my love for nonprofits, about abstract art, the grunge movement, and literature. When I would insert my thoughts about what they were talking about, I was met with either blank stares or fiery debates. I gave up and spent more time reading with my earphones on.

I felt so very conflicted. Stephen won awards and was motivated by the next one, he was on a leadership track, all of which was exhilarating for him. Because I was grateful and excited about his success (that was providing well for our family), I would somehow (I need a therapist to figure this one out still) find myself rooting for George H.W. during the 1994 election, going so far as to have a W sticker on the back window of my car (and having people flip me off or throw soda cans at me while driving). I was massively confused about who I had become.

Then we decided to build a new home, which, for me, provided a much needed distraction and life reset, or so I thought.

Why a new home? Everyone in our age bracket was doing the same thing. Moving out to the suburbs to design the life they wanted. Once again, I was conflicted. I loved our old home. It was built in 1924 and had been well taken care of and loved. I loved how it smelled at the beginning of summer, when the warm air would awaken the old wood - a smell you can't explain to anyone who hasn't lived in a hundred-year-old home. We had built-ins and buffets and cedar-lined closets that couldn't be replicated. But we did live in a suffering school system, and we were in our mid-thirties—the time, I suppose, that families consider their "forever" home. Stephen really wanted new. He wanted to be farther out into the country where everyone was building. The schools were rated excellent, the taxes were low, and the neighborhoods were booming. New pools, new trampolines, new shiny outdoor grills and John Deere riding mowers. Manicured half-acre lots lined with white picket fences. Utopia on a cornfield.

Yet, after the birth of our third daughter, Gabrielle, my desire to launch grew stronger. I shared my desire with Stephen, asked for his feedback on my ideas, and quickly realized we were not on the same page. Stephen didn't understand why I wanted to leave the security of my job and didn't appreciate my desire to do something to benefit more nonprofits in general. As a result, I began to retreat into my own head and slowly stopped interacting with Stephen, sharing new ideas, or asking for his input. This certainly didn't help our marriage.

I worried that Stephen wasn't paying close attention to our relationship and my retreat from it. We just kept soldiering on, playing the part. I also wondered if maybe I could actually do this playing-the-part thing. Maybe it would get better, or I would get more used to it. After-all, who is happy all the time? I began to play a percentage game. *What percentage of the time could I be unhappy? Or just mildly unhappy? Could I snap out of this? Live together under one roof but have separate lives?* What a miserable exercise that was.

Our last trip together was a few months later, in the late winter. I thought of it as an experiment. I would be open and accepting of what's possible and cognizant of what we could reconnect around. To my discredit, I didn't try very hard once we arrived. I felt, honestly, that the journey we were meant to have together had run its course and was complete. I remember walking for miles across a bridge in Key West, and for the first time ever, truly, it dawned on me that I didn't have to continue in this relationship. I was trying so hard to make everything work—our marriage, the outward perception to the world, my business, the girls' happiness—that I hadn't paused long enough to consider that if it wasn't working, I did have options. That, while not preferred, my life didn't have to feel this way, be this way. I didn't have to compromise if I didn't want to. And Stephen deserved this honesty.

On St. Patrick's Day, I came home and left Stephen. It was the hardest thing I had ever done, but the most important, for both of us and, most importantly, for our three girls.

My decision to divorce wasn't solely about my decision to become an entrepreneur. It had so much to do with so many things—obvious and nascent factors. And none of it was ideal. You enter into any partnership with the intention of realizing everything that it should be and could be. And then life gets messy and people change and desire different things for themselves, especially when you get married in your early twenties (define "self" at twenty-two). The idea or construct of marriage continues to evolve as humans evolve and as we live longer. A hundred years ago, "till death do us part" made perfect sense when you lived to forty, and when the little wife's sole purpose in life was to give birth, cook, clean, give birth, rinse and repeat. They had no idea there was more to living.

But the entrepreneurial side of the coin for women has been slow to evolve. And in fairness to men, so has men's ability to not only realize what was happening, but to catch up.

And so ensues the collision course. To be a man who is self-aware, secure and confident enough in their own skin, to embrace and support the career trajectory of their spouse is commendable. To find a man who is all of those things plus comfortable with their spouse being more successful (defined in many different ways) is like finding a unicorn. Or in my situation, like finding out that Jonathan is real.

Regardless, to stay in a situation that limits or jeopardizes you or simply makes the path harder toward what you aspire to do—what you know you need to do, must do, else your every waking moment from here on out will be filled with regret and resentment—was, for this woman and her daughters, not an option.

The only option was to begin this uncharted process of surrounding myself with unconditional supporters, everyday superstars, corny inspiring quotes, vulnerable situations, grace from above, courage from within, and a healthy dose of dumb luck from God knows where.

I do this for my daughters and your daughters. And their daughters. I write this to make sure they are all prepared, alert to the emotional risks and what might be lost during the "in between"—the time between resisting our evolutionary limitations, finally giving in to what your body and psyche have been saying all along, and saying yes to your crazy vision, while realizing the rest of the world might not have caught up to your bold vibe yet—the glorious but messy time when we prove to ourselves we knew what we were doing all along.

Once I moved forward with my divorce, I was ready to launch my business, full steam ahead, and one of the first things I reflected upon in that process was a bit of advice I'd been given when Stephen and I first decided to build our new home. Having grown up in the real estate and mortgage business, I found the idea of designing the inside of a home and picking out everything for the first time to be thrilling. But that feeling only lasted until it occurred to me that we had to borrow the down payment from my father and we would be doubling (or more) our current mortgage payment (plus utility bills, lawn bills, décor bills, and probably entertainment bills, for that matter). I began to worry that we were treading in water waaaaay over our heads, and that we had no business signing paperwork we weren't sure we could afford. Oh, and our friends questioned why our current neighborhood (and median house value) wasn't good enough for us any longer.

One day, I was sharing my *have-I-bit-off-too-much-?* fears with a woman named Marilyn, who was our CEO's executive assistant. Working within earshot and walking distance, Marilyn and I developed a mutual respect, and she also became my "work mom," if you will, looking out for me and offering sage advice when I needed it. In response to my panic the day before closing, Marilyn told me that this was the only way to evolve—that we needed to take on too much or push the limits of our budget and income, because, for most of us, that is how we then learn to drive harder, to ensure we can do what we say we would or make those new mortgage payments on time. **When we put a stake in the ground and outwardly claim it to be ours, it is fascinating how most of us will rise to the occasion and continue our career and financial mobility trajectories forward.** My house became a symbol of my growing desire to evolve personally and professionally. Because I willed it to be, it would work out.

In retrospect, I should have had Marilyn around me when I decided to launch. I could have used her perspective and it would have eased some of my new fears around not being ready, not knowing everything I should, and taking that next financial leap of faith in a way that was scarier than ever.

In fairness, however, I'm often asked a very practical question about this topic: How did you know that the risks you were taking would pay off? How did you feel comfortable enough that you weren't risking the farm? That your business model made sense, that the ramp-up time-frame wouldn't bankrupt you, that there was a market for what you were offering, and that you were positioned well enough to take a bite out of it?

This is one of the hardest questions I have to answer because I'm only now appreciating how it happened and why I felt comfortable leaving my nearly six-figure salary with benefits. There's no way you can truly know when you are doing it, just like you can never truly know when the right time is to get married, or have a child, or build a new house, or get a divorce. Possibly, there are more good vibes in your bones than bad ones? That the idea of saying *yes* doesn't make you want to throw up instantly? That the benefits outweigh the risks, or that you just know, more than you ever have, that this is your best shot at doing something you can't shake off? That if you don't do it, you'll... dare I say... regret it?

If we wait around for things to line up perfectly, we will miss the signs and opportunities that are out there, encouraging us, taunting us to say *yes.* We will go to our graves regretting or wondering or feeling incomplete. I would rather have tried and failed than the alternative. After all, we can control regret and avoid it completely (i.e., take no risks, stay within the comfort of our picket fence), but what we cannot control or get back are all the lost opportunities we miss when we say no to something that feels right. I credit this to the idea of "cumulative knowledge." A kind of sophisticated gut check that you acquire through years of learning and seeking and asking and failing. It's that inner voice and nagging feeling one gets when they know, despite the obvious reasons to walk away, that you have to say *yes*, and you'll figure out the details later.

In my line of work, that meant saying *yes* to my launch and knowing I would convince others to join me.

I can remember taking a call at our first office from an executive director of a national organization that supported public school foundations. We had blindly submitted a national conference workshop presentation per the "call for presentations" (we did this often in the beginning, hoping and praying for a bite), and he called me after 5 p.m. on a Friday, I think hoping to get my voicemail or something, but he got the real me instead.

Jim told me flat-out that he really liked our presentation pitch, and that he thought his members would dig it as well, but that he had never heard of us and needed to know more about why he should take a chance on our firm to deliver. My heart immediately began to race. I started to practice my breathing (so I didn't hyperventilate), and, as calmly as I could, admitted to being new but being well worth the chance; that we would pay our own way, didn't desire compensation, and so what did he have to lose? I also told him that I predicted we would do so well that he would be inviting us back for the next conference and be offering to pay our way and compensate.

He bit.

We've worked with that national public school association for several years, and I was their keynote speaker three years after my first trial workshop. We've also gained a reputation in the public school fundraising space and have helped many public schools go on to form foundations and impressive fundraising platforms. Sometimes it takes saying *yes* and working backwards to prove it. It also takes someone as kind and awesome as Jim to give those opportunities, which is why I try to pay this forward all the time.

As it turned out, we afforded the new house and all its additional expenses just fine. Marilyn was right. This new home would be where we welcomed our last beautiful daughter, but also where our marriage would come to an end. I often tell people that our perfect "picket fence" only went so far and I wasn't happy living within its confines. It didn't take me long to find an unhinged wood post, and out I bolted, bravely into the uncharted world. No more ideal blueprints and floorplans and shiny new appliances. I was happier operating as both architect and general contractor on a really small budget.

WHAT I *learned*:

- We are our own worst enemies.

- You've been practicing for this your entire life.

- No one has all the answers all the time, money, or support they need. No one. If you wait for the "right" time, you could wait too long.

- Defining the term "expert" is an art, not a science. Give yourself a break and call yourself one.

- Enthusiasm is contagious.

- Dream big and then say it aloud – you've just upped the ante on making your outsized vision a reality.

nine

THERE ISN'T ANY SHAME IN FAILURE, AS LONG AS YOU CONDUCT AN AUTOPSY

"The truth will set you free, but first it will piss you off."
–Gloria Steinem

Though my marriage ended in divorce, this, like everything else, became a learning opportunity. And to properly extract that learning, I needed to go back to the beginning. Way back, to early childhood.

Jaws came out in 1975, when I was three years old. Three. It was my very first movie and it scared the living shit out of me. Sitting in a crowded movie theater, being exposed to second-hand smoke (hell, maybe I was smoking, too), I watched my first full-length movie with my mom. Today, we laugh at how absurd this was, especially as our family vacationed in Florida a few times a year. I no longer, like millions of others, would enter the water. I'm not even sure I knew what an ocean was at that point, but I certainly wasn't going in one. Thanks, Mom.

The movie did leave another impression on me. As I grew up, I became fascinated by sharks. I would visit the library and take out book after book on sharks, memorizing each and every kind and classification. I would re-watch the first *Jaws* and watch all the subsequent ones (meh). Ultimately, a shark tattoo happened, as would giving my first born the middle name Quinn (one of the best characters ever).

As any seventeen-year-old in 1990, my first order of business, once my mom and grandparents dropped me off at art school, was to get a shark tattoo. Finally, I would be one with the most graceful, intimidating, and prehistoric creatures that ever lived. And like a careful rebel, I got my tattoo tucked neatly inside my panty line, so my king of the sea (or king of my ass) would only be known to those I deemed worthy.

While *Jaws* was my earliest memory of my mom, my second was even more life-altering.

Those smarter than me say the experiences that occur in a child's first five years of life are indelible and shape more of who we are than we would like to admit. For me, this ideology resonates. I believe my drive (and perhaps limiting beliefs) began around the age of four. One of my earliest memories casts a long shadow, as I let down the person who meant the most to me. My mom. Even as a small child, knowing nothing about the world and not intentionally creating the situation I found myself in, I knew I had failed my mom, and all I wanted from that day forward was to make it up to her. (And as a side note, I also know that had this memory – and watching *Jaws* – not been so visceral and violent, I don't think I would have remembered any of it at such a young age. But I did, and still do.)

Here's what I remember and what you need to know:

I have one sibling, a younger sister named Annie, and we are almost five years apart in age. Annie and I are spaced out that far because my mom had a miscarriage when I was a about four years old, which, as a result, nature required my parents to wait a bit before trying again and ultimately creating my sister.

As a first-born and only child at this point, I was completely self-absorbed and spoiled by the undivided attention from everyone and everything around me. Life was fairly predictable and structured. After my afternoon nap, my mom would religiously set me up with a glass of Tang, place cut carrots or apples in a bowl, and position me in front of the television to watch Bugs Bunny or another Warner Brothers show as a reward for being a good girl and napping. It was a two-hour cartoon love fest for me. Until my father came home, there wasn't much that could come between me and that television from 3 p.m. to 5 p.m. during the work week.

At the time, I'm sure it didn't register for me that my mom's attention toward me was different. It was being divided between me, a million other household tasks, and her growing belly. Perhaps I knew she was pregnant, perhaps I didn't. I honestly don't remember any thoughts about anything other than possibly needing a refill of Tang prior to hearing her scream my name over and over again as she began to miscarry her baby on our kitchen floor.

A good daughter of any age would tell you she had responded swiftly to her mother's calls for help, but I didn't. When I finally ascended the stairs from our basement TV room, I saw my beautiful mom on the ground in distress, her clothing and our floor smeared with this extraordinary bright red color—more vibrant than the red in my crayon box—with her arm outstretched, trying to reach the telephone installed at a six-foot-tall man's height on the wall, far too high for me to reach, or sadly, for her.

Like the red crayon that had somehow bled all over my mom's outfit, all I knew after a short forty-eight months on the planet was that when the Road Runner races toward and skids off the side of a cliff, careening to the bottom, the Road Runner gets right back up and his skinny legs convert back into racing wheels, and he's off.

What I was witnessing was also a cartoon. And because it wasn't real, I turned around and walked back downstairs to finish my carrots and TV show. The rest isn't in focus. My mom tells me she let me stay downstairs during the commotion that ensued, because that's where I needed to be, happily entertained, and she should never have called my name in the first place, placing me in an impossible situation. I felt bad for my response and what I did not do, knowing how silly it is to even type this. I was four.

But one of my first memories in life was so vivid and confusing and left me, once things came into focus for me, with an empty feeling that I didn't contribute. I let her down. Reflecting back, it does not surprise me that I've spent the rest of my life trying to undo this mistake and give my mother a different storyline about the kind of person I am.

Moreover, fast forward to my mid-twenties and my first and second born daughters are also spaced out close to five years apart because of a miscarriage I suffered in between them. I also divorced after sixteen years of marriage, like my parents. All of these things surely aren't coincidences, and it's fascinating to me to learn now what I couldn't see before; to understand how we repeat and recycle generational traumas. Stephen and I certainly drifted apart through a unique set of means of our own, but there are so many striking similarities between us and my parents—the miscarriage, the launch of my business, the timing of the divorce. This excavation of my past gives utility to my divorce as well as informs my future, as I can only become stronger as I continue to equip fresh insight about myself and why I make the choices I make. That's how we come to make better ones.

> **This excavation of my past gives utility to my divorce as well as informs my future, as I can only become stronger as I continue to equip fresh insight about myself and why I make the choices I make.**

With a fresh perspective, momentum, passion and forward-bearing motion, I embarked on my journey as an entrepreneur from a place of determination, not clouded by emotion. In honor of that, while some frame and hang their first dollar bill on the wall of their business, I framed and hung my first rejection letter.

Since the beginning, when we've lost a proposal or bid, I've always tried to see if the prospective client might be willing to tell us why, to provide us with some constructive feedback. I am the last person who thinks they are doing things the correct way (usually not), and often know I could be making things up along the way, or convincing myself during the pitch that I can do something I've never actually pulled off before (fake it till you make it), so I figure it never hurts to ask.

Alas, they don't usually share why. Now, if I ask during a phone conversation, there's a better likelihood I'll get some feedback, but even then, it's usually a safe answer: "The committee made the decision," (meaning they, personally, had nothing to do with it, sure). "We went with someone local/we went with someone who was not local," etc. But every so often, someone will tell us something we need to hear—something that we probably already know is a weakness or glitch, but it takes a stranger to affirm and give us that swift gut punch that we deserve. And for that, I am always grateful.

I was only about two years into our firm when I worked tirelessly to get a local nonprofit with a big reputation to select us for their feasibility study. I saw it as an amazing coup that would provide us with a feather in our cap and would signal our growing capabilities. I had worked with the leadership team and many of their board members and had been a small donor to their mission for several years. I was simply crushed when they selected a big national firm to do the work.

What I learned from that experience, and from the honesty of my internal lead contact, was priceless. I printed out the email they wrote in response to my questions of "why" and had it hanging on our wall until we met all three challenges, as follows:

- You don't have a national reputation.
- You don't have enough experience.
- You don't have enough internal bandwidth.

Did I tell you about the time my ex-husband told me I couldn't run a half marathon? *Game on.*

And these three reasons, all of which were fair and reasonable at the time, were now my *raison d'être*. I would work relentlessly to identify what our national milestones should be (inclusion into The Giving Institute, requests for interviews by the Chronicle of Philanthropy), what "enough experience" looked like (a combination of more than two years under my belt plus a deeper client base with major campaign successes), to defining bandwidth for our firm (adding a new advisor and operations and marketing team member).

To this day, I thank that nonprofit for honestly sharing with me what their search committee thought at the time. Today, I would offer some of those "advantages" that they saw with a mega national firm over a local specialized firm were superficial and didn't serve them any better than we would have (and also would have saved them a whole bunch of money in the end). But at that time and place, I didn't know this, and I did need to have my ego and reality bruised a bit.

I took down the email after we checked all the boxes, but still have it in safe keeping. As I write this, I realize I have a new email with a new list of things to prove wrong that needs to be placed in a frame and hung. I miss that fire in my belly and focus in my intention to improve.

You will never, ever be 100% ready to launch. And frankly, by design, we shouldn't be. Part of the entrepreneur "chip" is reconciling at once this constant struggle between perfection and spontaneity. Structure and fluidity. This dance we agree to participate in, often solo, of seeming like we have our shit together when, internally, we are questioning *every. single. thing.* Be vulnerable enough to ask for constructive and respectful feedback, and then do something with it—don't be afraid of it! Be grateful to be told you aren't ready yet, and then use that as fuel to prove someone wrong. In the end, you'll need a few pairs of running shoes (and Band-Aids and gel packs), ladies, as this is definitely a marathon, not a sprint.

WHAT I *learned*:

- Be vulnerable and brave enough to ask "why" something didn't work out your way.

- Keep what you learn about failure front and center and as a constant reminder until you've fixed things.

- **Prove your detractors and challengers wrong** in the most positive and passionate way possible: by thanking them for caring enough to tell you the truth.

- **Teach your team that to fail is to learn.** Show me someone who doesn't fail and I'll show you someone who doesn't take enough risks.

ten

KNOW WHEN YOUR TANK IS EMPTY
(AND BE CAREFUL WHAT YOU REFILL IT WITH)

*"The final forming of a person's character
lies in their own hands."*
—Anne Frank

"I don't know how she does it." Ever had that said to you before? Infrequently is it said as a compliment. If ever, it's a backhanded one, it's aim our fragile and guilt-ridden egos.

I've always thought that statement and all the fanfare surrounding it was code for: you make me look like a slacker, would you please stop? But I'll tell you, after a few years post-launch, I think there's value in actually breaking that question down. *How does she do IT?* Well, what is *it?*

It is that magical mojo you'll generate internally and exude externally. That special power that will turn you into a magnet, attracting unique opportunities and influential people your way. That air of ease and patience you project into the ether that creates calm and confidence in those around you. That energy that never seems to stop.

Until it does, and it will, and your tank will be E.M.P.T.Y. Now what are you going to do? We both know you are not going turn back or give up—not now, not ever. You are going to have to find yourself a healthy, sustainable outlet, my friends.

In the beginning, it feels like you have to just keep pushing and pushing and pushing and doing whatever it takes to make your business sustainable, and to some degree, that's true. But you can't run a business on fumes, **because your business is only as strong as you are** in the beginning, so making sure that you are engaging in activities, in thoughts, and with people who fill you up is crucial. This means that my schedule looks really packed, but some of the things on my schedule are important to the maintenance of my own mental, physical, and psychological health, because there is always time for those things (as long as you're willing to admit to and cut the minutia we subconsciously dedicate ourselves to).

A friend of mine once said to me (in a snarky tone), "How do you find the time to work out?" and I looked at her and replied, "How do you not?" From there unfolded, on her end at least, a Battle of the Busy. She sought to prove to me that she literally had not a minute of extra time. She detailed how many afterschool activities her children had signed up for (Really? They signed the paperwork?), how ineffective and disengaged her spouse was (I don't have one to begin with), and how much her co-workers counted on her to be present during the workday so, in turn, they could model her same behavior to their employees (Stockholm Syndrome, anyone?). Next, she took out a beautiful violin and began playing it. There wasn't a dry eye in the house. Except mine.

We are prisoners of our own limiting beliefs!

I challenged her that if she gave me permission to evaluate her weekly schedule and commitments, I would create for her (careful that I didn't say, "Find for her...") two hours of available time to fill with whatever personal aspirations she wanted to take on. But I offered that she needed to be honest with me about said commitments and appointments and routine, plus be willing to let go of 25% of them.

Many of us have dug ourselves into about a six-foot deep rut that we can no longer see a way out of, so we justify our reality. We normalize our routines and we actually roll around in our own shit (when it works for us), believing that we are SO BUSY we can't do anything for ourselves any longer. And we wonder why we drink too much, why our di-

> **We all waste about 25% of our time doing things that don't matter and no one would miss if we cut them out.**

vorce rates are so high, and why we wake up resenting the life we created—one that is no longer joyous. But only we can make the hard changes necessary to create this space so that we can be our best selves again.

For the first few years of my business, I would mark any non-work appointments I had made during the course of the workday as private or I'd use a fake code word for them. My Pilates or tennis or hair or nail appointments would all be given pseudonyms because I worried that if my other team members (we all have access to each other's calendars) saw that I was taking a break during the day to do something non-work related, they might think that I was slacking, or I feared setting a bad example and then they, too, would get their nails done at 2 p.m. or, God forbid, take an early morning yoga class.

We all had an agreement from day one that our children's doctors appointments and Christmas shows and teacher conferences were all acceptable to prioritize during the workday, because almost all of my team works evening hours at least a few times a week—our clients hold their board meetings after work or we make presentations to prospective clients in the late afternoon, and so forth. Plus, as we all are becoming acutely aware, the start and finish of a workday is quickly eroding. No matter the industry, the expectation is that we are constantly responsive. We must work hard to manage, from the beginning, a new client relationship that puts parameters in place. Otherwise, we are all at risk for the late night text or email from a client needing our advice right at that very moment.

In my opinion, however, I feel like the benefit of being always "on," or at least in "monitoring mode," as we refer to it at our firm, is that we can schedule a haircut or yoga class during the day. We've earned that right to manage our own schedule and our own deliverables. **My job is not to micromanage or question how a highly skilled, educated, and career-motivated team member is clocking their hours. All I've ever cared about is that they do their work to the satisfaction of our client and to the quality standards of our firm. Plain and simple.**

The burnout rate in advising, whether it be our variety or the accounting, legal, or financial advising fields, is excessive. One of the main reasons that professionals are attracted to being an advisor (or consultant with a firm) is that there's this romantic notion about "being your own boss" (without all the hassle of actually being one), managing your own schedule, and generating (and being highly incentivized for) your own book of business and managing those client engagements in a way that reflects and leverages your own professional style and energy. And every bit of that is true. But when you think about doing that for a small handful of clients, it seems like a dream come true. When the expectation of your employer (yep, don't forget, you aren't self-employed) is that you do that with eight to ten clients at any given moment, well, it takes an incredibly structured, resilient, and deeply motivated person to thrive versus burn.

One of the ways our most successful advisors achieve that thrive zone and learn that, indeed, being an advisor IS the single best way to love what you do while not jeopardizing your sanity or those around you, is to take time out for yourself as often as you can and whenever you can. There are weeks and months where I feel I have a slight sliver of extra time so I might book a yoga or Pilates class back-to-back for a few days. Why? Because next week (or the following several), I will go completely without. I'll be lucky to brush my teeth, let alone work out. Or because for the past few days I've been working until midnight, so I feel a little less guilty about starting my day with a desperately needed manicure.

"God is in the details."
–Ludwig Mies van der Rohe

Remember, God is in the details. And my God often looks like a glass of wine at 4 p.m. with a friend, or a tennis match on an early afternoon in the most beautiful part of fall. There's nothing that can recharge my batteries better than the euphoria I feel being active outside. The ideas that I can generate on a brisk walk or on my yoga mat are more innovative and creative than I'll ever produce sitting behind my desk at 3 p.m. Ever.

Life is too short, and our passion for what we do cannot be contained – or sustained – through an eight-hour workday.

There is also nothing that can recharge me more on a business trip than a really nice hotel. Yes, I said business trip. When one travels often, we give up a lot. We miss kids' games or art classes, dinners out with our spouse or friends, or simply our own bed and shower. Because I ask this of my team, and of myself, the last thing I'm going to then ask them for is to save me a few bucks and stay at a marginal hotel. If I'm not willing to do this, I certainly am not going to ask it of them. Many of my team look at this kind of overnight travel as a getaway (especially those of us with young kids), a peaceful break in the noise and chaos that can be home. Plus, a nice dinner and glass of wine. Trust me, a few extra bucks in this line item yields personnel dividends for years to come.

I cannot underscore how many friends, or stories of other entrepreneurs I've been told, who did not find their healthy outlets and did not have friends who challenged them to create a path toward balance, and who crashed and burned as business owners. If there is ever a time that you will be at your lowest point of energy, questioning all that you've done and wondering why you can't seem to find results quick enough, it will be as you launch your business.

There will be a fork in the road as you begin this journey.
One path will take a lot of work, it will require you to look outwardly, like you are being selfish and putting yourself before other others in your life. This path will sustain you, however. It will give you energy, clarity of mind, and joy. You will be the kind of person who others want to be around. The other path will require very little work and inconvenience, but it will drain you and others around you. It is the path so many take— becoming bitter, resentful, inactive, and/or gravitating towards easy highs, like alcohol or prescription meds, to coat that uncertainty you'll feel. It's an easy path, but very few who take it are successful for long. And it doesn't matter if you are launching your own business or if you work in a high burnout profession, like advising.

No matter the path you ultimately choose, do me a favor and don't share the process and angst you went through to get there with your staff. I know that sounds like a crazy statement. *Who the hell does that?* Um, a lot of you will be tempted to. You'll be working late with someone and just gush all the shit that's going on with you. Or you'll come in early like a tornado and plop down in the staff meeting and over-share. I beg you, resist the urge. This is not the place nor the right people (despite the fact you spend more time with them than your family, they are not your friends, do not confuse the two). Why not, you ask? Especially if these are people who you courted into a (hopefully) long-term professional relationship, people who would follow you off the proverbial cliff? That's your answer. The image they've created of you needs to stay intact for them. Find your posse, your Army of Misfits, your dog, I don't care – anyone but the people who have made the commitment to believe in you and your vision.

I encourage my team, and you, to own the time you take for yourself. **No apologies,** no marking those appointments private (I've since stopped as well, but I do have a conversation with each new employee about how we earn this right and how they can, too). Identify and create the space for you. No one else will, and, in the end, you'll be able to do the same for those who join your team. You'll speak from a place of experience and you will stand out from your competition.

WHAT I *learned*:

- Exercise and personal growth activities will be your biggest ally against fatigue and stress and burnout.

- Don't ignore the signs that you need to take time for yourself and don't apologize for doing so.

- Don't take the easy route and numb or medicate your stress and fears.

- **Share with your posse about the way you feel, but don't do the same with your staff.** Separate life and work. They need to see you as the badass you are, even when you are faking it. No one wants to work for a whiner.

- **Upgrade your hotel room every once in a while.** If it started your morning out with a jump in your step and you rocked your presentation, ten years from now, I promise you, the extra $100 won't make a damn bit of difference.

conclusion
just the starting line

"Times, they are a-changing."
–Bob Dylan

his winter, I decided to take up teaching again. It was something I loved to do as a graduate assistant and as a guest professor here and there. I love a college campus and the thirst for knowledge it exudes, and was courted not by my alma mater, the University of Toledo, but by a neighboring rival school, Bowling Green State University, who has a nationally recognized entrepreneurship program in their B-school. I was elated and honored to be asked to teach their *first-ever* women and entrepreneurship class – *score!*

As any type-A would do, I prepared extensively for it: drafting and re-drafting a syllabus, researching data and lining up guest speakers for months in advance. As it drew closer to the first week of class, the assistant dean informed me that there were six students registered, which, for a first class, was both a strong showing and better for me as I would be teaching new material and getting used to the flow and format and routine of the college world.

To illustrate how life continues to stay messy, dirty, and un-scripted - but in new and different ways - I had quite a curveball thrown at me on the first day of class. After arriving early to get everything ready, I took a seat behind my desk and waited for my students to arrive. Much to my surprise, student number one arrives and is male. I thought, *Damn! That's awesome. How cool is this kid? Someone raised him right.* And then student number two sauntered through the door. Again, a male. *Well, I'll be! I'm impressed, BGSU. You are producing some woke ass students.*

And then student number three, number four, number five, and number six all arrive. Yep, you guessed it. All males. My women and entrepreneurship class is officially 100% male. I wondered if I was being punked. I wondered what the ridiculously small odds were of this hap-pening. *Should I buy a lotto ticket on the way home?*

(As it turned out, there was an explanation. Before I was recruit-ed to teach this class, the slot was held for a social entrepreneurship class and, for higher ed bureaucratic reasons, they were unable to update and replace the class title with mine. And to make matters worse, somehow, the communication of said small detail was lost down the same bureau-cratic black hole.)

As the last student took his seat, my head was racing: *Am I in the wrong class? Will they all drop once they know what I'm teaching about? Will I need to revamp my material?* All my limiting beliefs came flooding back, pinning me up against a wall inside my head. In what seemed *like an eternity,* but probably lasted all of sixty seconds, I reclaimed my will to succeed, collected my confidence and thoughts, and just like when I accepted my Entrepreneur of the Year award two years ago, I laughed at myself. But this time, out loud.

That, my friends, is the difference. **Ten years ago, I didn't have the courage to own my feelings, and now I do. And so will you.** You will fake it till you make it and you'll navigate swimmingly through the mucky grey seas.

And not only did none of my students drop the class, we actually picked up another student! You guessed it – another male. All seven of these students are amazing. Not only do I have an unbelievable story surrounding my first women and entrepreneurship class, I also have an incredible group of young men who are genuinely interested in learning about what it's like to launch a business as a female. We constructively and respectfully challenge everything, even the fundamental premise – how much is truly unique to a female, and how much might be a shared experience regardless of gender?

On the surface, there seems to be many similarities – struggles and wins – experienced universally by either gender. But then there is this irrefutable and sobering fact that is uniquely female: despite year-over-year growth in women-owned businesses (114% over the last twenty years versus the national average growth rate of 44% for businesses overall[1]), there is a massive gap in female versus male entrepreneurial *financial success*. Keep reading…

While exclusively female-owned businesses now total 39% of all U.S. businesses[1] (which sounds like kind of a big deal, right?), the devil is always in the details. Of those fierce female-owners, here's how the money shakes down:

- We only generate 4% of the total business revenue[1] (for dramatic purposes only, that means 96% of business revenue in a massive marketplace is generated by male-owned firms).

- And of that paltry figure, only 1.7% of us generate $1M or more in revenue annually[1] (I think this is known as statistically insignificant or *margin of error* in some circles).

When I asked my students what this means they were a) super kind (or super strategic) to first congratulate me on being in the 1.7% and b) puzzled. *How could all this growth and energy not equal revenue?*

While this book is not an optimal forum to debate all the possible answers to this question, I implore you to do so on your own, with your friends, your children, or over a glass of wine or cup of coffee with a successful business owner of any gender. This is our next hurdle, girlfriends – soon it won't be good enough to simply encourage women to launch. Instead, for those of us who desire it, we must also pave a path, widen the lanes, and remove some ugly orange barrels to allow for financial parity as well.

In the meantime, don't let excuses stand in your way. No matter how old you are – 20, 37, or 82 – pave that path like you are working with a bulldozer, no matter if you are 100% ready or not. Your energy, enthusiasm, and can-do attitude will determine your success or failure, *not someone else.* So ditch your naysayers, find that Army of Misfits, and bless and release those limiting beliefs.

You are as powerful as you believe yourself to be. End of story.

[1]American Express. *The 2017 State of Women-Owned Businesses Report.* Commissioned
by American Express. American Express OPEN by Ventureneer; CoreWoman.
2017. Retrieved from https://about.americanexpress.com/sites/americanexpress.
newshq.businesswire.com/files/doc_library/file/2017_SWOB_Report_-FINAL.
pdf

aly sterling

ABOUT THE AUTHOR

Long before Aly Sterling founded her eponymous consulting firm, she was solving the unique yet similar problems encountered by nonprofit organizations.

Her decision to start her own business in 2007 was driven by her belief in leadership as the single most important factor in organizational success, and her determination to work with multiple causes at one time to scale societal change.

Today, Aly manages the direction and growth of her firm while advising clients on the organizational challenges that affect their sustainability and mission success.

In 2015, Aly led her firm to membership in The Giving Institute, an exclusive and highly respected professional organization for nonprofit consultants. The Giving Institute is best known for publishing the annual Giving USA report – and today she also serves on the Giving USA Foundation board.

Aly's expertise includes fundraising, strategic planning, search consultation and board leadership development for the well-positioned nonprofit. She is regularly sought for comment by trade and mainstream media, including the Chronicle of Philanthropy and U.S. News & World Report. She has contributed to publications of BoardSource and The Governance Institute, as well as The Giving Institute. Her workshops and keynote presentations have been featured at the meetings of the National School Foundation Association, the Association of Fundraising Professionals, Habitat for Humanity, Boys & Girls Clubs of America, and a variety of foundations around the country.

Aly is an alumna of Leadership Toledo, a recipient of the *20 Under 40* award and a Women in Communications Crystal Award winner. In 2018, she was inducted into the Northwest Ohio Entrepreneurial and Business Excellence Hall of Fame. Aly holds a master's degree from the University of Toledo and is a fellowship graduate of the executive leadership program at Case Western Reserve University's Weatherhead School of Management. Most recently, she earned certification in the 21/64 approach to working with multigenerational families with funds, foundations and other family enterprises.

Aly serves on the board of trustees for St. Ursula Academy and the Arts Commission of Greater Toledo, as well as the advisory board for the University of Toledo Family Business Center. Aly is past president of the Northwest Ohio chapter of the Association of Fundraising Professionals and has served on the boards of Leadership Toledo, David's House and Advocating Opportunity, an organization formed to stop human trafficking.

Aly currently serves as an adjunct professor at Bowling Green State University, where she teaches about women and entrepreneurship.

ALYSTERLING.COM